A History of Gloucester Prison, 1791-1950

Jill Evans

ISBN: 978 1 5454 7984 1

Published by Glos Crime History Books
31 Court Road
Newent GL18 1SY

Cover illustration: A row of cells in an upper tier of A Wing, Gloucester Prison. (Jill Evans, 2017)

CONTENTS

PREFACE

I first became interested in the history of crime when I studied the subject as part of a Master of Arts degree in History with the Open University. As I live in Gloucestershire and have a particular interest in local history, I wrote my dissertation on 'Female Offenders in Gloucestershire, 1750 to 1850'.

After finishing my degree, I continued to study crime and punishment in Gloucestershire, for my own enjoyment. This research led to my first book, *Hanged at Gloucester*, being published by The History Press in 2011.

When Gloucester Prison closed down in 2013, it seemed to me that it would be a good idea to write a book about its history. However, I came to realise that although I had accumulated a respectable amount of material on the prison from my previous studies, a great deal more research would be needed before I would be ready to write a comprehensive history of the prison. In addition, many of the records for the more recent years of the prison's existence will remain closed for some time.

It is my intention in the future to produce a weighty volume, covering every aspect and all eras of the prison's history, accompanied by multiple contemporary illustrations and extensive notes. In the meantime, this is my offering: A brief history of Gloucester Prison, its staff and its inmates, concentrating on the years up to 1950, and illustrated with some of my own photographs, taken between 2013 and 2017.

INTRODUCTION

During the 1770s, prison reformer John Howard made a tour of all the prisons in England and Wales. In 1777, he published his findings in *The State of the Prisons in England and Wales*. A second edition of his work was brought out in 1780, and a third followed in 1784. The terrible conditions he described in the nation's gaols raised public awareness of the plight of prisoners and calls for action. Many local prisons were rebuilt or improved as a result of Howard's publications.

In Gloucestershire, Howard had visited the city and county gaols in Gloucester and the houses of correction (also called bridewells) at Cirencester, Lawford's Gate (in North Bristol), Berkeley, Winchcombe and St Briavels. The city gaol, which held prisoners whose offences had taken place within the city walls, was the responsibility of Gloucester's aldermen, and they decided to build a new prison in Southgate Street, which opened in 1782.

The county's gaol and houses of correction were all administered by the magistrates who met at the County Court of Quarter Sessions four times a year. The county gaol had been housed for centuries in the keep of Gloucester's castle. As well as holding criminal prisoners (most of them waiting to be tried, transported, or executed, or being held because they had not paid a fine), it also held debtors and acted as the county house of correction, for prisoners convicted of misdemeanours.

Howard recorded that the gaol was in a considerable state of disrepair and that lack of usable space meant that all types of prisoner were kept together. In particular, there was no proper separation of women from men, which had resulted in 'licentious intercourse between the sexes', and the birth of several children who had been conceived in the gaol. There was only one courtyard for all the inmates to use, and no bath. Due to the unhygienic and overcrowded conditions, many prisoners had died of smallpox and gaol fever.

The Gaoler had no fixed salary, except for £10 per annum for running the bridewell section. His income was made up by charging the inmates fees. He also had a licence to sell beer in the prison. A chaplain was paid £40 a year for attending the gaol, but he rarely made an appearance. There was no prison doctor, but a local surgeon or apothecary would be sent for by a magistrate, when required.

Some improvements were made to the castle gaol in response to Howard's findings. However, Sir George Onesiphorus Paul, who had become the High Sheriff of Gloucestershire in 1780, believed that complete reform of the county's penal system was required, and this could only be achieved by building a new prison.

In March 1783, Paul was the foreman of the Grand Jury at the Gloucestershire Lent Assizes. This afforded him the opportunity to address many of the county's noblemen and gentry, and he made a speech in which he reviewed the problems identified by John Howard, namely the unsafe and insecure building in which prisoners were kept, the lack of separation of the sexes and of the different classes of prisoner, and the unhealthy environment in the gaol, caused by the cramped and dirty conditions.

At the next Assizes in August, Paul noted that some improvements had been carried out at the old gaol, but, he said, because of the increasingly ruinous state of the building, all prisoners were being kept together at night, in 'one dark pen', measuring twelve feet by eleven feet, and they had to be chained to the walls to prevent any escape attempts, as well as to keep men and women apart.

This speech resulted in a meeting of the county's nobility, gentry and clergy, which took place on 6 October 1783. Paul proposed the construction of a new county gaol, penitentiary and house of correction in Gloucester, in the grounds of the castle. In addition, three new houses of correction would be built at Horsley, Northleach and Littledean, and the existing house of correction at Lawford's Gate would be rebuilt.

The cost of all the building works would be borne out of the county rates. An action group was established and it was decided to secure a private Act of Parliament to achieve its aims. In the meantime, a petition was sent to Parliament concerning the problems of overcrowding and gaol fever at the current gaol.

In January 1784, a gaol committee of sixteen persons started to draw up the details of a bill to be submitted to Parliament. It was intended that the new prison complex in Gloucester would house a total of 207 inmates. Thomas Cook was chosen to be the builder, and William Blackburn was to be the architect. Blackburn was very interested in penal reform and had already designed a number of prisons with the purpose of employing the separate system advocated by John Howard.

The Gloucestershire Act (25 Geo. III c.10) passed into law in 1785. The Act specified that the new prison must separate, day and night, males from females, debtors from criminal prisoners, the untried from the convicted, etc, etc. There must be individual night cells for all prisoners, work cells, refractory cells (for punishment), and a separate section for those acting as witnesses for the prosecution. There should be a 'plain and decent' chapel, infirmary apartments, baths, places for purifying clothes and airing yards, officials' apartments, and a lazaretto (where incoming prisoners could be quarantined until they were passed as disease-free).

Rules for the new prison were to be drawn up covering all aspects of its running. The Michaelmas meeting of the Quarter Sessions each year was to appoint two magistrates, who were to visit the prison at least three times a quarter (known as Visiting Justices), and report their findings to the court of Quarter Sessions, noting any problems. The Quarter Sessions was to appoint a governor who would be in overall charge of all the different parts of the prison. In addition, a salaried chaplain and surgeon should be employed, who would take care of the spiritual and physical well-being of the prisoners.

Building work began in 1787, with the prisoners remaining in the castle gaol until the new prison was ready. A rule book was drawn up in 1789 and published in 1790. This was a comprehensive work, detailing the classification of prisoners, the duties of officials, the behaviour of prisoners and how the troublesome could be punished, the use of irons and fetters, diet, work, dress, etc, etc.

In the last week of July in 1791, the prisoners were transferred from the old gaol into the new prison complex. Building work had not yet finished, but the institution was now considered to be usable. At the meeting of the County Quarter Sessions in January 1792, Sir George Onesiphorus Paul announced that all the building works were finally completed.

1

THE PRISON BUILDINGS

The new prison complex consisted of a gaol, a penitentiary house, and a house of correction. The whole site, covering about three acres, was entered through a gatehouse, situated on the east side of the complex. The gatehouse (also known as the entrance lodge) was run by a porter, who had rooms in the building. The other rooms in the gatehouse were designed to receive new prisoners, including bathrooms and lazaretto rooms, where they could be kept before being medically examined. The gatehouse had a flat roof, on which executions of county prisoners were to take place.

The main building inside the prison was three storeys high, and held the gaol on one side and the penitentiary on the other. Both sections had separate areas for men and women. In the centre of the building there was a chapel and an infirmary. The gaol had dayrooms, night cells and airing yards for each category of prisoner. In the penitentiary section, it was intended that the inmates would have both a day cell to work in and a night cell to sleep in, so there were fifty-two each of day and night cells.

In 1812, James Neild, who had followed John Howard in making a tour around all the local prisons, published *The State of the Prisons in England, Scotland and Wales*. In the section entitled 'Gloucester County Gaol and Penitentiary House annexed', he gave a detailed description of how the prison looked at the time of his visit, which took place ten years before his work was published.

At the front of the prison, he said, was the 'Turnkey's lodge' [the gatehouse]. The ground floor held a fumigating room, a guard-room, and a pantry, a bakehouse and warm and cold baths. Upstairs were two rooms to store flour and wheat, four lazaretto cells, two rooms for prisoners' clothes, one for irons, locks, bolts, etc, and the porter's bedroom.

On the outer gate there were two donation boxes, one inscribed 'To encourage Penitence and Orderly Behaviour in Criminal Prisoners' and the other 'For the Relief of Poor Debtors'. The flat roof of the gatehouse, used for executions, had a bell placed between two chimneys, which was tolled 'during the awful ceremony'.

Neild was able to look inside the governor's accommodation, which he described as 'the Gaoler's house'. On the ground floor, there was a Magistrates' Committee Room, and a kitchen, pantries, and a brewhouse, with cellars underneath. On the floor above was a sitting room and two bedrooms, and above that a dispensary, infirmary rooms, and a general hospital room. On the upper storey was a 'foul ward', with three cells for prisoners with infectious disorders.

The prisons, he said, were 'surrounded by eleven separate courts, of an irregular polygon shape'. The fences between each court were made of open wooden palisades, to allow a good flow of air between them. To discourage conversation between the classes, there was a small garden border in front of each fence. There was enough room between the courtyards and the main boundary wall to have a garden, in which vegetables were grown.

Within the gaol section of the prison complex, there were several 'spacious and dry' courts for felons, with arcades, and dayrooms for each class, 'fitted up with every convenience for simple cookery'. The ground floor of the penitentiary had three courts, joined by two passage-ways, containing a total of twenty-six work cells, which were heated by underfloor brick flues. The prisoners slept in single cells, which measured eight feet by six feet, and were well ventilated.

The chapel was described as 'a neat building'. Each class of prisoner had a separate door through which to enter. Prisoners could see the other members of their class, but no-one else, except the chaplain.

The laundry was situated in the female section of the penitentiary, because the women did the majority of the washing for the prison. The works-section, supervised by the taskmaster or manufacturer, had a shop from which finished goods were sold, several workrooms, and a storeroom for materials and tools.

Altogether at the time of Neild's visit, there were 178 sleeping cells, plus two 'refractory' cells (dark rooms used for punishment), which were 'dark indeed, but, like the rest, well-ventilated'.

In 1826, major alterations were started at the prison, to the designs of John Collingwood. The perimeter wall of the prison complex was extended eastwards, along the side of Barbican Road, so that the original gatehouse was now contained within the prison's walls. Construction began on a new gatehouse, in the north-east wall. This was two storeys high, with a flat roof, as before. A self-contained Debtors' Prison, three storeys high, was built to the east of the original buildings. It is likely that the octagonal structure on the south-east corner, later attached to the governor's house, was constructed during this building phase.

The death of an inmate at Northleach House of Correction in 1842 led to a government inquiry being held to investigate the conditions and management at all of the county's houses of correction and the county prison. The report of the Inquiry Commission was laid before Parliament in February 1843, as were subsequent reports of the Government Prison Inspectors and the Government Prison Surveyor. All criticised the county prison and the houses of correction for being overcrowded, not dividing the prisoners into their proper classes, and the want of proper ventilation and heating in them all.

The report strongly recommended the closure of all the county's penal establishments and the construction of one large, central prison, which would house all the prisoners from around the county. The chairman of the County Quarter Sessions, Purnell B. Purnell, objected to this idea, pointing out to his fellow magistrates that the cost of carrying out these recommendations was estimated at approximately £120,000.

He suggested an alternative plan. The houses of correction would be altered and extended, and would be used to hold prisoners sentenced to imprisonment for three months or less. As for the county prison, a new building would be constructed within it, designed to be a Separate Prison for male convicts, run on the same type of separate system as was in operation at the recently-opened penitentiary at Pentonville, in London. The prison complex would be divided into five distinct sections: Debtors; Gaol; Penitentiary; Separate Prison; and Female Prison. The whole complex would be called 'Gloucester County Prison'. The cost of the scheme was estimated at £27,000.

These proposals were unanimously adopted at the Quarter Sessions in January 1844, and at the subsequent Easter meeting, it was announced that the government had approved the plans. Building work began soon afterwards, to the designs of Thomas Fulljames, the county surveyor.

In order to create the new prison block, two wings, three storeys high, were added to either side of the original gatehouse entrance, and a new chapel was built at its back, which connected the new building to the old gaol and penitentiary. The new prison building could hold a total of 141 prisoners.

In October 1850, it was announced at the Michaelmas Quarter Sessions that the building works at the county prison were complete, at a cost within the original estimate. The magistrates, accompanied by members of the press, were invited to inspect the new buildings. A reporter from the *Gloucester Journal* gave a detailed account of what he observed on his visit.

On entering the main prison complex, the magistrates and members of the press passed through a corridor which divided the wings of the new prison and opened onto a spacious 'piazza', upon the columns of which stood the new chapel. In the central entrance block, spiral staircases led to the two upper floors. There were rooms for warders situated by these staircases on each floor. Outside the building, to the left and the right, there were airing grounds for the prisoners.

Each wing of the new block contained three tiers of cells. The two upper tiers were surrounded by galleries, reached by iron staircases, and lighted by windows sunk into the vaulted roof. In the end wall of each wing was a large, arched window. The windows in the cells were glazed with thick, waved glass, high up in the wall, preventing the prisoners from seeing out.

The 1790s gatehouse entrance, incorporated into the Separate Prison, with A Wing to its left and B Wing to its right. (Jill Evans, 2013)

Moving into the chapel, it was described as a square apartment of considerable size, 'cheerfully lighted by long, circular-headed windows'. The size of the new chapel meant that all classes of prisoner could now attend services at one time, without detriment to the system of separation. The seats in the chapel were divided into four hundred boxes, one for each inmate. The rows of seating were steeply tiered, so each occupant was looking over the head of the person below. Because of this, the prisoners could see only the minister and officers, not each other.

The party then visited the 'victualling department', which had an engine room, containing a steam engine, with two boilers embedded in the brickwork, which was used for cooking, washing and warming the gaol. Next to the engine room was a spacious kitchen, containing a row of copper boilers, in one of which soup was being boiled by a jet of steam.

Concluding their visit to the new buildings, everyone moved along a dark passage into the old prison complex, and entered the penitentiary. The reporter believed that this range of buildings, with its cells opening onto outside walkways, had 'the air of a pleasant old mansion'.

At the same time as the Separate Prison was built, new accommodation was provided for the governor in the centre of the complex, between the new prison and the old buildings and overlooking the airing yards. This meant that when anyone wanted to visit the governor in his home, they had to be escorted through the prison to reach him.

In 1863, it was decided that a new house should be built for the governor, with an entrance outside the prison walls. An advertisement appeared in the *Gloucester Journal* on 13 June 1863, inviting builders 'to tender for the erection of a Governor's Residence', which was to be built 'in connection with the present Octagonal Building, at the South East Angle of the County Prison'.

The new house had its entrance on Commercial Road. Its gardens were divided from the prison grounds by a high wall, but the governor could keep an eye on what was happening in the yards from a large window on an upper floor at the back of the house.

On 1 April 1878, the government took over the running of all local prisons, under the supervision of the Prison Commissioners, and Gloucester Prison became 'Her Majesty's Prison Gloucester'. When the transfer took place, the chairman of the Quarter Sessions reported that they were handing over a prison capable of accommodating 377 inmates (327 male and 50 female), 'with all necessary requirements of reception, dark, padded and other cells, stores, officers' quarters, etc, complete'.

The first report of the Prison Commissioners, published in November 1879, revealed that while there was plenty of accommodation at Gloucester, not all of it was in a good condition, commenting that although a great number of the cells had been improved in the penitentiary, the whole building was 'utterly unfit for the modern requirements of a prison'.

In 1904, the female prison closed down. In the 1920s, most of the remaining parts of the original (1790s) gaol and penitentiary were demolished, when work began to build a terrace of eight houses for prison officers. These were constructed at the west side of the prison, facing the Quay. These houses were in turn demolished in 1985, when a new reception and administration block was built in the north-west section of the complex.

The 1980s reception block and entrance, with part of the older boundary wall. (Jill Evans, 2013)

2

THE PRISON SYSTEM

The separation of prisoners into different classes was fundamental to the new prison system at Gloucester. This meant not just the separation of male and female prisoners, but that untried felons were kept apart from convicts, criminals from debtors, and, ideally, first-time offenders from 'old lags'.

The 1790 rules divided the prisoners into eleven main classes. In 1808, when Sir George Onesiphorus Paul devised new rules, the number of classes was kept the same, but some of the descriptions were changed and extra sub-divisions were made within some classes in the gaol.

In January 1809, in a speech he made at the Epiphany meeting of the Quarter Sessions, Paul revealed that putting his original scheme into practice had proved difficult, largely because of the number of classes into which the prisoners had to be divided. The need for all the different divisions had meant that in most sections of the prison there had been a problem with overcrowding, and in some years there had not been enough cells to cope.

In 1802, Paul stated, there had been forty-three male convicts occupying thirty-two cells in the penitentiary. This had resulted in the closure of the house of correction section, so that the penitentiary could gain more cells. Prisoners committed to the house of correction by county magistrates were sent to Northleach from then on. As for the female convicts, the greatest number held had been seventeen, but there were only twelve cells for them. A group of six cells from another division had been annexed to solve this problem.

Overcrowding had been far greater in the gaol, in particular in the time shortly before the Quarter Sessions and Assizes. The greatest number of male inmates held at one time had been one hundred, but there had been only forty-six cells to hold them, so they had to be put into other parts of the prison, out of their classes. Regarding the female prisoners, there had been thirty of them at one time, but only twelve cells to hold them.

Moving on to prisoners who had been condemned to death, there were twelve cells provided for them, but after one Assize there had been twenty-two prisoners. The fines had four cells, but on one occasion there had been sixteen people in that class. Like the felons, they had to be housed in other parts of the prison. The only section which had not had problems with overcrowding was that of the debtors. Paul concluded that the prison coped well during ordinary times, but not under extraordinary conditions.

In March 1811, Paul gave evidence to a House of Commons Committee, chaired by G. Holford, investigating the running of the penitentiary houses in the country. When Gloucester Prison first opened, the sentences of male penitentiary prisoners had been divided into three, progressively more lenient, parts. The Committee was interested to hear why this system subsequently had been abandoned.

Paul explained that the system had been dropped within five years of Gloucester Prison opening. This had been due largely to the advice of the chaplain, who argued that once a man had completed the most severe part of his sentence, in which he worked in solitude, and had moved into a more lenient phase, where he worked with others, all the good which had been achieved initially was quickly lost. In its place, a regime which was somewhere between the strictest and most lenient stages of the progressive system had been adopted for the whole of a prisoner's sentence.

In 1819, Paul and governor Thomas Cunningham gave evidence to another House of Commons Select Committee, this time investigating the state of the country's gaols. Cunningham was asked about the dropping of the three-stage system, and he said he agreed with the chaplain that the good effect of solitary work in the first stage was lost when men worked with others in the later stages.

It transpired that the governor had come up with his own system for inmates who were sentenced to one month's imprisonment. They were not given any work to do during their time in the prison, but had to sit in solitude in their cells, and take their exercise alone. They were fed on bread and water, with a pint of 'pease soup' twice a week. Cunningham asserted that no-one ever came back to prison for a second time after that. When Paul was asked if he knew about this, he said he did, and that the solitude was relieved by attending morning chapel and evening parade.

Concerning the numbers of prisoners, Paul reported that at that time, the capacity of the gaol was 137 night cells, while in the penitentiary there were 66 night cells and 49 work cells, plus three other communal work rooms for male prisoners, and two large rooms and a 'wash-house' for females. Overcrowding meant that male felons were being put in cells of different classes at night, including the condemned cells and infirmary, and even then there was more than one prisoner to a cell.

On 16 December 1820, Sir George Onesiphorus Paul died. In the following years, his version of the separate system was largely abandoned. In 1823, a new Gaol Act was passed, which was the first in a series of legislation by which the government increasingly took control of the supervision of local prisons. Further legislation in 1835 led to the introduction of government Prison Inspectors, who were to visit all prisons and report back to the Home Office.

The 1835 Prison Act advocated a more severe system of separation in penitentiaries, based on the regime used in American prisons, by which the prisoner worked, ate and slept in the same cell, spending most of the time in solitude. At Gloucester, this new system was not adopted in its entirety, because of its use of the treadwheel as the main form of hard labour. However, in 1837 new rules were introduced at the prison, which stipulated that penitentiary prisoners must 'preserve complete silence at all times, and have no communication by signs, word or deed with other prisoners'. Prisoners could communicate with an official or officer, but only if absolutely necessary.

From 1844 to 1850, a new 'Separate Prison' was built at Gloucester, intended to house convicts and to be run on the latest version of the separate system. This building was constructed in order to appease the Home Office, which had been threatening to have the prison closed down.

Only a few years after these major alterations had been made, the 1853 Prison Act was passed, which provided for national convict prisons to hold those sentenced to a minimum of three years of 'penal servitude'. This meant that prisoners serving sentences at Gloucester Prison were no longer called 'convicts', the maximum prison term they could be serving was two years, and none of them had been found guilty of committing the most serious categories of crimes.

Men who were sentenced to penal servitude by the Gloucestershire courts were sent at first to Wakefield, Millbank or Leicester prisons, before being transferred to Pentonville. Women were sent first to Millbank, then went to Brixton Prison.

New sources of inmates were soon found to fill Gloucester's ample accommodation, as various other prisons closed their doors. Tewkesbury's Borough Gaol closed down in 1854, and prisoners from that district were sent to Gloucester. The county prison had been taking in some Gloucester city prisoners since 1846, and in 1858 the city gaol closed down completely. By 1860, all four of the county's houses of correction had been converted for other purposes and the prisoners who used to be sent to them went into Gloucester Prison instead.

On 1 April 1878, when Gloucester Prison became 'Her Majesty's Prison Gloucester', its administration ceased to be the responsibility of the county magistrates, and the cost of its maintenance was removed from the county rates. The court of Quarter Sessions continued to take an interest in the prison's affairs though, receiving quarterly reports from the Visiting Justices, the governor and other prison officials, as previously, and discussing the annual reports of the Prison Commissioners.

At the same time as the government took over the running of local prisons, a progressive stage system was introduced. There were four stages, with the first, at the start of the prisoner's sentence, being the most severe. Prisoners could be promoted into the next, more lenient stage by earning a certain number of marks, which were awarded for completing daily work tasks, but they had to spend at least twenty-eight days in one stage before being able to progress. At each stage, the prisoner could earn an increasing amount of money (to be paid at the time of release), and 'perks' such as borrowing a library book, being able to send and receive a letter, or seeing a visitor.

The progressive system was intended to encourage hard work and good behaviour, but in practice, most prisoners at Gloucester were serving short sentences, often of no more than a month, and so rarely had the chance to pass beyond the first, most severe, stage. This meant that prisoners were kept in solitary confinement and performing hard labour for six to ten hours a day, and for the first fourteen days of their sentence, they had to sleep on a hard plank bed.

This system was still in operation in 1906, when William Sparrow, who had served two months with hard labour at H.M.P. Gloucester, gave an interview on his release to the *Cheltenham*

Chronicle (1 September 1906). He described how difficult it was to sleep on a plank bed with no mattress for the first fourteen days, and how he had worked on his own in his cell, sewing mail bags. After a month, he had progressed to the next stage and had been allowed to borrow a library book.

In June 1904, the female section of the prison was closed down and H.M.P. Gloucester was designated a 'subsidiary prison for convicts'. In October of that year, it was reported at the Quarter Sessions that Gloucester had received convicts from Portland, Parkhurst and Dartmoor, who were housed in a wing of the Separate Prison. The convicts sent to Gloucester from those prisons were serving the final parts of their sentences. Prisoners from Manchester and London also had been transferred to Gloucester.

There were always far more 'local prisoners', who either were waiting to be tried or had been sentenced at the Gloucestershire courts of Quarter Sessions and Assize, than convicts sent from other prisons. The 1906 Annual Report of the Prison Commissioners stated that in October that year, Gloucester Prison held 107 local prisoners and 37 convicts.

In 1922, Worcester's County Prison closed down. By that time, Worcester held prisoners from Herefordshire as well as those from its own county, as Hereford Prison had closed in 1915. It was decided that Worcester's prisoners would be divided between Birmingham and Gloucester, depending on the district which had committed them.

In the first decades of the twentieth century, rehabilitation and training became key components of a prisoner's sentence. The

1920s saw the introduction of voluntary teachers coming into prisons, including Gloucester. The need to entertain long-term prisoners was recognised, and carefully chosen lectures, concerts and plays were given occasionally. Prison visitors were also introduced, to give inmates the opportunity to talk to somebody one-to-one who was outside of the prison system.

In May 1946, the prison governor, Colonel Northfield, gave a talk to the Gloucester Branch of the National Council of Women. Northfield told the audience that the main purpose of the prison administration now was 'the successful re-establishment in life and outlook of the prisoners, with effective appeal touching their higher qualities to become better citizens'. Encouragement was given to useful, constructive work. This included 'good reading, provision of evening classes, contact with the outside world through voluntary visitors and the wireless, periodical debates and good music'.

Unfortunately, despite these innovations, the period after the Second World War saw a large increase in the prison population, leading to overcrowding at all the country's prisons, including Gloucester. The design of the Victorian structures, purpose-built to keep prisoners in isolation, was inadequate for the modern system. At Gloucester Prison in the late 1940s, in some sections there were three men sharing a cell designed to hold one person. When protests were sent to the Home Office, the reply was that the situation was the same in prisons all over the country, and no lasting solution was found.

One of the serpent-shaped brackets underneath the galleries in A and B Wings. Above them, the bases of the rail posts are in the form of lions' paws. This symbolised justice controlling sin. (Jill Evans, 2017)

3

OFFICIALS & STAFF

The Governor

When Sir George Onesiphorus Paul had discussed his plans for a new prison in the 1780s, he had stressed the need for a competent governor to be appointed, who would oversee the running of all the various sections of the prison. While the old gaol-keeper had earned most of his money by charging fees to prisoners, it was decided that the new governor was to be paid a salary of £200 a year, and he was to receive a share of any earnings from work done by prisoners. However, he had to give a bond to keep the rules, or pay a penalty which was the equivalent of one year's wages.

In the 1790 rules, the duties of the governor were listed. He was to keep a journal and a punishment book, both of which had to be available for inspection by the Visiting Justices. He was to attend chapel every day, and take prayers if the chaplain was absent. After chapel, he should do the roll call and then distribute the daily allowance of bread to the prisoners. During the day, he should see every prisoner at least twice in every twenty-four hours, and visit every part of the prison to check security and see that all was running correctly.

In 1808, when the rules were revised, the duties of the governor were: to see all prisoners once every twenty-four hours; attend chapel and take prayers if the chaplain was not there; call roll, examine the cleanliness of prisoners and see the bread given out; go round the prison once a day; see the beds were made; watch for escape preparation; and visit anyone in the refractory cells. He was to see that the turnkeys did their work and was not to absent himself from the prison overnight without the permission of a magistrate.

The first governor of the new prison was William Cunningham, who was appointed at the meeting of the Trinity Quarter Sessions in July 1790. Paul, who made frequent visits to the prison, quickly became dissatisfied with Cunningham, as he did not seem to understand the rules that he was supposed to enforce and was too lenient with the prisoners.

In October 1792, William Cunningham fell ill. His son, Thomas Cunningham, who was the keeper of Horsley House of Correction, stood in at Gloucester during William's indisposition. Paul took the opportunity to correct his mistake in hiring William Cunningham in the first place, by keeping Thomas as the governor at Gloucester and sending William to replace his son as keeper at Horsley.

Thomas Cunningham proved to be a much stricter governor than his father, and was less popular with the prisoners because of this. He had particular trouble with the debtors, who were not bound by the same rules as criminal prisoners and resented his attempts to impose any discipline upon them.

In 1836, after over forty years as governor, Thomas Cunningham died. His replacement was Captain Mason, who was elected by the court of Quarter Sessions from a short-list of four candidates. The first fifteen years of Mason's tenure went well and in 1851, he was given a testimonial by the Visiting Justices for his good service. In the years following, though, the magistrates became less satisfied with Mason's leadership.

Mason finally resigned in December 1861, after twenty-five years as governor. In his letter of resignation, he said that the 'confinement and labours involved in the duties of his office, in addition to his advancing years, had suggested to him the course he now adopted'. At the meeting of the Quarter Sessions in the following January, it transpired that Mason had been about to be put under investigation over an 'incident' at the prison, but his resignation meant that the matter was dropped.

The next governor was Captain Cartwright, who was at Gloucester from 1862 until he resigned in 1869. The Visiting Justices reported to the Quarter Sessions that they had received Cartwright's resignation with regret, 'as they had ever found him a most intelligent, humane and efficient officer'.

When the position of governor was advertised in the newspapers in October 1869, the salary offered was £400, with 'house, fuel and light'. Candidates had to be under forty years of age, and it was suggested that experience of the separate system would be useful. The successful candidate was Captain Henry Kenneth Wilson, who was at Gloucester until 1874, when he went to be governor at Maidstone Prison.

The Prison Governor's house, Commercial Road, built in the 1860s.
(Jill Evans, 2017)

Wilson was followed by another ex-army officer. James Knox started at Gloucester in July 1874. He was a captain when he came to Gloucester, but had become Major Knox by May 1879. At the time of his appointment, he was thirty-seven years old. After leaving the army, he had worked for four years at the Kingswood Reformatory for Boys. Knox was at Gloucester Prison for nearly twenty years, until in December 1893, he gave notice of his intention to leave, in order to take up the position of governor at Leeds Prison.

At the meeting of the Quarter Sessions in January 1894, it was written in the minutes that the court wished to record 'their high estimation of the manner in which Major Knox has always performed his duty, and their appreciation of the care and kindness which he has shown for the prisoners under his charge, and the efforts he has made for their future welfare'.

Knox was an ardent teetotaller, and treasurer of the Gloucester branch of the Church of England Temperance Society. He was a firm believer that abstinence from alcohol was the best means of reforming criminals, and once described Gloucester Prison as 'Her Majesty's Temperance Hotel'. He left Gloucester to take up his new post in May 1894.

With the departure of Knox, it was decided to follow the national trend of having a 'Chief Warder in Charge' instead of a governor. Mr James Keech became the head of Gloucester Prison under this title. When he retired in 1899, he had been in the prison service for thirty-five years. When Keech left, the experiment of having a Chief Warder in Charge instead of a governor ended.

Mr John Finn became Gloucester Prison's new governor in the year 1900. He had the dubious distinction of being the man in charge when five men escaped from Gloucester Prison in 1906, after locking him in a cell and stealing his watch. Finn left Gloucester in 1910, when he went to Cardiff Prison as governor.

Finn's successor was Captain Herbert Marwicke Atherstone Hales, who was Gloucester's governor from 1910 until 1915, when he rejoined the Gloucestershire Regiment to serve in the First World War. Hereford Prison closed down in 1915, and its governor, Mr H.T. Pearce, was transferred to Gloucester in Hales' place. Pearce moved to Cardiff Prison in 1919.

The next governor was Mr Harry Whyte, who was at Gloucester for ten years. He left in 1929, to replace Mr Pearce as governor at Cardiff. Mr W. Foster, who succeeded Whyte, came to Gloucester after being the Deputy Governor at Brixton Prison. He was at Gloucester for six years, transferring to Lincoln Prison in 1935.

Mr Sidney T.E.P. Ennion, who took over as governor in Foster's place, came to Gloucester from Liverpool Prison, where he had been the deputy governor. He was only at Gloucester until 1937, when he moved to Chelmsford Prison. His replacement was Captain H.G.H. Evered, who had been the deputy governor at Wandsworth Prison. He was at Gloucester until 1940.

Mr E.E. Brindley became the new governor of Gloucester Prison in June 1940. Brindley had worked his way up through the ranks, starting his career in 1908, as a warder at Liverpool Prison. In 1933, he went to Leicester Prison as Principal Officer, then came to Gloucester as Chief Officer in 1936. In 1938, he transferred to Pentonville as a First Class Chief Officer, spending two years there before he came back to Gloucester as governor.

When he retired in August 1945, *The Citizen* reported that Brindley had been responsible for many innovations at Gloucester, 'all intended to humanise the prison experience'. He had been governor through most of the duration of the Second World War, which had been difficult because of staff shortages, food rationing and blackouts. A local magistrate and prison visitor commented that Brindley was 'one of the best Governors we have had at Gloucester Prison for many years'.

Brindley was replaced as governor by Lieutenant-Colonel Edward Walter Northfield, known as 'Colonel Northfield'. He had come to Gloucester from Wandsworth Prison. Before joining the Prison Service, Northfield had enjoyed a distinguished military career, spending seventeen years in the Middle East. Whilst serving in Transjordan, he had become a close friend of the ruler, his Highness the Emir Abdullah, and became his personal aide-de-camp. Northfield remained at Gloucester until 1952, when he transferred to Leeds Prison.

The Chaplain

The 1790 rules detailed the duties of the prison chaplain. He was to take prayers on Wednesdays and Fridays, preach a sermon on Sundays, and hold communion as often as he thought fit. He was to keep a journal, attend any prisoner who asked to see him, and circulate religious books.

The chaplain had a vital disciplinary role in the prison, as he had the power to endorse punishments given out by the governor. He visited troublesome prisoners and offered them advice on their future conduct. He signed certificates of good behaviour for orderly prisoners who had finished their sentences.

He was a frequent visitor to any prisoners who had been condemned to death, offering them spiritual comfort, but also trying to get them to admit their guilt and name any accomplices. On the days when executions took place, he held a special chapel service, and he accompanied prisoners to the scaffold.

At the old castle gaol, the chaplain had been the Revd James Evans. Paul decided to dispense with his services when the new prison opened, and replaced him with the Revd Edward Jones, who was a canon at Gloucester Cathedral. His salary was £40 per annum. Jones remained as prison chaplain for thirty-one years, retiring in 1822.

The next chaplain was the Revd Robert John Cooper, the son of magistrate Richard Bransby Cooper. He proved to be another long-serving official, staying at Gloucester for twenty-eight years. He retired in August 1850, when faced with the possibility of losing the services of an assistant chaplain, as he didn't feel able to cope with his duties without help, at his time of life.

Cooper's replacement was the Revd John Francis Herschel, who was at Gloucester for the relatively short period of seven years. When he left in 1857, an advertisement for a new chaplain was placed in the *Gloucester Journal*. The successful applicant would be required to take morning and evening services and preach a sermon twice every Sunday, and on Christmas Day and Good Friday. He would have to attend the prison daily to read morning prayers, visit the sick and see those in solitary confinement, instruct prisoners in classes and provide religious and moral instruction to all inmates.

The chosen candidate on this occasion was the Revd L.A. Dudley. He stayed at Gloucester until November 1865, when he resigned, citing ill-health. The next chaplain, the Revd H.G. Layton, came to Gloucester from Aylesbury Prison. He was at Gloucester from 1866 until 1878, when he transferred to Maidstone Prison. Layton's successor was the Revd G.H.

Fletcher, who was at Gloucester until June 1883, when he moved to Manchester Prison. Fletcher was followed by the Revd James Hart Johnson, who came to Gloucester from Wandsworth Prison, where he had been the assistant chaplain. He was at Gloucester for fourteen years.

In 1897, a local clergyman was appointed as the new prison chaplain. The Revd James Hughes Owen had been the vicar of St Paul's Parish Church in Gloucester since 1894. He was also the chaplain of the Provincial Grand Lodge of Gloucestershire Freemasons, and President of the Gloucester City Cycling Club. He was prison chaplain until his death, at the age of sixty-six, on 26 March 1908. He was buried at Gloucester Cemetery, after a service at St Paul's Church.

Hughes Owen's replacement as prison chaplain was another local clergyman, the Revd William Christian Macklin, who was the vicar of St Mary de Lode in Gloucester. He was described in the local press as 'the second city incumbent to hold the prison chaplaincy'. Macklin was at Gloucester until 1922.

The Revd W.G. Pritchard became prison chaplain in place of Macklin. He took a great interest in the rehabilitation of prisoners after they left gaol, and became the Honorary Secretary of the Gloucestershire Prisoners' Aid Society. He resigned from both roles in April 1939, after sixteen years as prison chaplain.

The final three chaplains in the period of this study were: the Revd Charles Stuart Donald, who was at Gloucester from 1939 until 1942; the Revd N.W.J. Kent (who was also the vicar of St Stephen's Parish Church), from 1942 to 1947; and the Revd Dennis Daven-Thomas, who was still the chaplain in 1950.

The Surgeon

In the new prison, a surgeon (later called the medical officer) was employed on an annual salary. The 1790 rules stipulated that the prison surgeon should visit the sick every day and see every prisoner twice a week. This was no doubt more medical attention than most inmates ever received outside the prison. He also examined all incoming inmates in the gatehouse, to check they had no contagious complaints, before they went into the main prison.

The prison surgeon, like the governor and the chaplain, was required to keep a journal. The entries in this journal reveal that his role extended beyond treating the sick. He commented on the cleanliness of the bedding, the ventilation in the buildings, and the state of the sewerage system and the water supply. The surgeon was responsible for deciding when the fires should be lit in the winter, and he could order extra food and clothing for inmates if he felt they needed them.

The prison's first surgeon was Thomas Parker, who was employed on a salary of £38 a year. He often made comments in his journal about the running of the prison, and especially its lack of cleanliness, which annoyed the governor. He remained at the prison for twelve years, until his death, on 19 July 1803.

The next surgeon was John Pleydell Wilton, who was employed on a salary of £47 a year. Wilton was at Gloucester for nearly thirty-six years, but after 1812, he was often unwell and unable to attend to his duties. His son (J. Wilton) or one of his apprentices stood in for him during those times.

Wilton died in June 1839, and was replaced by Thomas Hickes, who was already familiar with the prison, having acted as its surgeon during Wilton's last illness. Hickes remained at Gloucester for thirty-five years. In June 1874, he notified the authorities of his intention to retire by the end of the year. The *Gloucester Journal* commented: 'No man in the medical profession is more popular; and we hope that when Mr Hickes shall think fit to relinquish his active duties, there will be a long period of pleasant retirement for him to enjoy.'

In August 1874, an advertisement appeared in the newspapers, stating that the office of Surgeon at Gloucester County Prison would become vacant around Christmas time. The annual salary offered was £175. Applicants had to be under forty years of age and properly qualified. There were thirteen applications for the position, and Mr H.E. Waddy was the successful candidate. He had been an assistant surgeon at Gloucester Infirmary.

Waddy was the prison surgeon for eleven years, handing in his resignation in August 1885. His replacement was Dr Oscar William Clark, who was at Gloucester for nearly twenty-eight years. Clark died suddenly in June 1913, while he was carrying out his duties at the prison. He was known to have had a weak heart.

Dr James Adamson Bell was announced as the new prison medical officer in August 1913. He remained at Gloucester until 1929, when his place was taken by Dr Edward Graham, who had been the deputy medical officer at the prison. Dr Graham was still at Gloucester in 1950.

Male Staff

When the new prison opened, the most important member of staff after the governor, chaplain and surgeon, was considered to be the taskmaster, who was also to act as the deputy governor. The 1790 rules stated that a taskmaster (also known as the manufacturer) was to be employed, on a salary of £50 per annum. His main job was to find work for prisoners, buy any necessary tools or materials, and supervise the labour of the prisoners. He had to be able to keep accounts, and he was to act as deputy to the governor, when needed. The 1808 rules summarised his duties as being to act as first assistant to the governor, to purchase materials, supervise work, keep accounts, and sell any goods made.

The first taskmaster was William Green, who had been a debtor in the old castle gaol. Paul found him to be careless over security (a prisoner escaped thanks to a rope and tools not being put away at the end of the working day) and slack in keeping his accounts. He was dismissed in 1796 and the governor took over his duties for a while, until a replacement could be appointed. This was probably Samuel King, who was the taskmaster in 1799, according to entries in the governor's and Visiting Justices' journals.

The role of deputy governor later became separated from that of taskmaster, but it continued to be combined with another job at the prison, perhaps because a deputy was only needed when the governor was away or indisposed. In March 1847, Thomas Moore was described as 'the clerk and deputy governor', when he was dismissed by the court of Quarter Sessions. Moore had got into trouble after the matron refused his request to bring a female prisoner into one of the yards used by the males, saying it was against the governor's orders. According to the *Gloucester Journal*, Moore had said, 'the governor be d-----, who the d---l cares about the governor?'. He went on to make other remarks about the governor to the Visiting Justices, which he later retracted.

The chairman of the Quarter Sessions regretted that Moore had to be dismissed, because he had been 'a long servant for the county, and a very good one. He was an excellent accountant, and had been of the greatest possible use to the present governor'. He was dismissed all the same, and his job was advertised in April 1847, with a salary offered of £120 a year.

The appointment of Moore's replacement caused a disagreement at the Quarter Sessions. The magistrates voted to appoint a Gloucestershire man, Henry Morland Jeens, as the new clerk and deputy governor. Jeens was a competent accountant, but he had never worked in a prison. The Board of Visiting Justices refused to accept his appointment as deputy governor, because they wanted to take on someone who had experience of the separate system in operation at Pentonville, which would be used at Gloucester when its new Separate Prison building opened.

A compromise was agreed, by which Jeens would be offered the job of clerk, and a new head officer of the Separate Prison would be appointed, who also would act as deputy governor when required. Mr Duncan Stuart was taken on at Gloucester in this role. He remained at Gloucester Prison until 1858, when he was appointed governor of Swaffham House of Correction in Norfolk.

An advertisement was placed in the *Gloucester Journal* in April 1858, inviting applications for the post of 'Head Officer at the Separate Prison (which forms one of the departments of the County Prison)', who would also act as Deputy Governor when the Governor was absent or ill. The salary offered was £100 per annum, with 'clothing as at Pentonville Prison', and apartments with fuel and light. Previous experience as a 'Disciplined Officer at a Government or other Separate Prison' would be considered an advantage. Applicants were not to be over forty-five years of age.

It isn't known who was appointed on this occasion, but five years later, in January 1863, the position of Head Officer of the Separate Prison and Deputy Governor was advertised again, this time with a salary of £105 per annum on offer. The successful applicant was named (like the first taskmaster) William Green. In 1871, Green applied for a raise in his salary, to which the magistrates agreed. He remained at Gloucester Prison for another seven years, until in April 1878, he was appointed as governor of Maidstone Prison, in Kent.

After the government took over the administration of Gloucester Prison, the position of deputy governor appears to have been dropped, as it was not included in the list of staff given in the Prison Commissioners' Report of 1878-9.

Another important member of staff was the porter (or gatekeeper), who lived in the gatehouse and was the first point of contact for anyone coming into the prison.

It is known that the name of the porter in 1800 was John Manns, because a female convict accused him of 'annoying' her. Her claim was dismissed, but the governor removed Manns' set of keys, as this wasn't the first time there had been a complaint against him. In 1809 the porter was named James Cope. His wife was the prison matron. Sir George Onesiphorus Paul disapproved of Cope because he was a Methodist and he didn't attend the prison chapel services.

The porter from about 1831 was Richard Lock. A former soldier, Lock was 'pensioned off' in 1850, after having a leg amputated. Because he lived at the gatehouse, losing his job meant losing his home too. In the summer of 1850, he wrote a letter to the court of Quarter Sessions, informing them that his wife was dying and begging that he might be allowed to stay in his accommodation for a while longer. This request was granted. At the following Quarter Sessions in October, the court discussed the amount of pension Lock should receive, and it was decided to award him £12 per annum, for his nineteen years of 'faithful servitude'.

Lock's replacement was Daniel Wait, whose wife was employed too, as the searcher of new female prisoners and female visitors. Presumably Wait wasn't at the prison for long, because in 1872, when 'gate porter' William Elliott resigned due to failing health, he had been the porter for twenty-one years, so he must have started the job in around 1851.

When the prisoners moved into the new prison in July 1791, the magistrates decided that the governor could employ a 'nightguard', if he thought it necessary, until all the building works had been completed. The works were finished in January 1792, but one night in July of that year, three prisoners escaped, so it was decided that a permanent night watchman should be employed. An unnamed person in that role was dismissed in July 1803, after he refused to continue working at the end of his shift and was said to have been impertinent.

The employment of a night watchman was included in the new rules which were devised in 1808. His role was to patrol the yards at night, twice every hour. His rate of pay was two shillings and six pence a night. It was now specified that the night watchman should never work shifts in the prison during the day. In 1808, the watchman was called John Brown. He was implicated in aiding the escape of a prisoner and subsequently was tried at the Assizes, where he was acquitted.

By the early 1870s, it was the custom at Gloucester Prison for three special officers to be employed as night watchmen. However, at the Quarter Sessions meeting in March 1873, it was decided that the number of watchmen should be reduced to two.

During the day, the prisoners were supervised by prison officers, who were originally called 'turnkeys'. This reflected the main part of their job in the early days, which was to lock and unlock the many cell doors and gates in the prison. Later, turnkeys were renamed warders, and after that, prison officers.

The 1790 rules allowed for the employment of only two turnkeys, one on a salary of £30 per annum, and another, if needed, at £25 per annum. Their salaries were paid a half year in arrears, to ensure their good work. The ability to write and to do small sums were requirements of the job. In 1808, when new rules were drawn up, the only change made concerning the number of turnkeys was that the Quarter Sessions could decide on how many needed to be employed.

An original cell door, with its lock removed, in the Victorian prison block. (Jill Evans, 2013)

In 1811, when Paul gave evidence to the Holford's Committee, he said that the prison only required two turnkeys and a porter in normal circumstances, but needed to take on an extra man just before the Quarter Sessions and Assizes, when there were more prisoners in the gaol than usual. An example of this occurred in January 1819, when the governor informed the Visiting Justices that he needed extra help to cope with just over two hundred prisoners then in custody. He was told to take on the keeper at Shire Hall as a temporary measure.

Later in 1819, Paul gave evidence to the Select Committee investigating the gaols. He stated that at that time, there was one turnkey in the gaol and two in the penitentiary, plus a porter and a night watchman.

By the mid-nineteenth century, more warders were being employed at Gloucester, to supervise the different sections of the prison, and the lesser rank of 'under warder' had been created. In February 1852, an advertisement appeared in the *Gloucester Journal* for two competent persons to act as under-warders for 'the separate department of the prison'. Candidates had to be between twenty-one and thirty-two years of age, and they would have to reside in the prison and wear a uniform. The salary offered was £40 a year.

In July of the same year, a similar advertisement appeared, again for an under-warder in the Separate Prison. The age range this time was between twenty-five and thirty-five years old. It may have been that one of the successful applicants for the positions advertised in February had proved to be inadequate, because the advertisement this time added: 'No person will be considered eligible who does not understand the Separate System of Prison Discipline.'

Staff members regularly were required to take on a number of roles within the prison. In June 1867, an advertisement appeared in the newspapers for a 'trade instructor in mat-making and weaving', who also would be given 'occasional disciplinary duties'. In September of the same year, the prison was advertising for two competent persons as under warders, who would act in turn as 'Night Patrols'.

By the time that the government took over the running of all local prisons in 1878, a hierarchy of staff had developed, with the governor at the top, followed by various grades of warder. This gave prison workers the opportunity to have a structured career, and the possibility of promotion to a higher rank. A good example of this is shown in the career of Giles Cambridge, who started at Gloucester Prison in 1858 as the Second Treadwheel Officer, then became the First Treadwheel Officer in 1860. A year later, he became Head Officer of the Gaol, then in 1871, he was promoted to Principal Warder.

The hierarchy also meant that warders could be disciplined by being demoted to a lower rank. This happened in 1861, when it was discovered that prisoners had been let out of their cells to visit the water closets, then allowed to return without supervision, which had led to prisoners visiting each other in their cells. It was decided that Principal Officer Ursell was most to blame, and it was recommended by the Visiting Justices that he should be demoted to the rank of Treadwheel Officer of the Penitentiary.

Despite the increase in the number of staff employed at the prison, at times concerns were raised that the number of male officers was insufficient. In 1850, when a prison inspector came to look at the new buildings and alterations which had been made, he aired his concerns that the thirteen male staff then employed at Gloucester were not enough to maintain order.

Such misgivings were repeated in October 1906, when eleven convicts got out of their cells after overpowering two prison guards, and five of them escaped from the prison. This episode led to questions in the House of Commons about staffing levels at Gloucester, considering that as a subsidiary convict prison, a section of its inmates were 'hardened criminals', but the Home Secretary felt that the number of staff was sufficient.

During the Second World War, there was an inevitable shortage of prison officers, as those who were fit to do so joined the armed forces. In May 1941, the Prison Commission placed advertisements in the local newspapers, for 'temporary (War Auxiliary) men officers at H.M. Prison Gloucester'.

By the middle of the nineteenth century, Gloucester Prison was employing schoolteachers. In the early years of Gloucester Prison, any instruction of prisoners was carried out by the chaplain and was concentrated on studying the scriptures and religious works. During the nineteenth century, the government brought in a series of regulations requiring prisons to provide classes in elementary education, and school teachers were employed to do this, under the supervision of the chaplain.

In 1871, Gloucester Prison's schoolmaster William Davis resigned, at the age of seventy-four. He had been at the county prison for thirty-two years. He gave up his position because of declining health, and only lived for two more years after his retirement. By July 1874, the schoolmaster was Arthur Evans, who had been in the prison service for ten years, having previously worked as a messenger. In that year, he applied to the Quarter Sessions for a raise in salary, which was granted.

In the 1840s, the prison's accounts had been the responsibility of the clerk, but in March 1872, an advertisement appeared in the *Gloucester Journal* for the position of Prison Accountant, which was a post 'previously held by Mr Samuel Mayer'. The successful applicant's duties would include 'to check the daily, weekly and other Dietary Books, the Quarterly Accounts, attend Shire Hall two days preceding Quarter Sessions, and examine and check the accounts of the Keepers, etc, etc'.

In October 1872, the prison advertised for a Clerk and Store-Keeper, 'to replace Mr Henry Morland Jeens, deceased' (who had been appointed as clerk in 1847, but not as deputy governor). He would be required 'to keep the books and accounts, weigh out supplies, etc, etc'.

In March 1873, the Quarter Sessions discussed the position of Mr John Palmer, who had been appointed as the prison clerk on a trial basis at the last meeting. It was decided that due to his inexperience, he needed longer to learn his duties, so his probationary period was extended. In the meantime, he would be assisted in certain duties by the schoolmaster.

The *Gloucester Journal* of 7 August 1920 reported that Mr W.T. Reed had retired from the post of chief clerk at the prison, after thirty-six years in the prison service at Gloucester. The newspaper commented that Reed was 'always courteous and of a genial disposition', and that he 'had won the confidence, respect and esteem of his superiors, his fellow officers, and all with whom he came into contact'.

Female Staff

When the original rules for Gloucester Prison were published in 1790, the only female employee mentioned was a sutler, who was someone who would bring provisions to sell to prisoners. It was suggested that it would be preferable if this person was 'an elderly woman'. There was nothing in the rules concerning the employment of a woman to supervise the female prisoners.

By December 1800, a Mrs Kent was employed at Gloucester in the role of 'assistant to the governor in the female penitentiary'. At that time, it was discovered that one of the female prisoners had been involved in helping Mrs Kent to smuggle soap out of the prison, in order to sell it. Mrs Kent also had caused prison jackets to be cut up or destroyed, and sheets to be divided up to widen other sheets or to be made into aprons, without permission. After an investigation, she was dismissed.

When the rules were revised in 1808, it was stipulated that a salaried matron, under the governor's authority, was to be in charge of 'linen, laundry, female work and clothing, and beds'. At around that time, the matron was Mrs Cope, who was the wife of the porter. She died in July 1811.

According to an entry in the Visiting Justices' journal on 18 October 1845, the matron, Mrs Susan Peel, had been dismissed, after it was discovered that female prisoners had been making caps, collars and shawls for her, which she sent to London (where presumably they were sold). There had been other occasions where Mrs Peel's work had not been satisfactory, including one incident earlier that month, when she had left the doors open between the male and female sections of the penitentiary.

An advertisement for a new matron was placed in the *Gloucester Journal* in November 1845. Applicants had to be able to read and write, as they would have to keep a journal. General knowledge of the management of a similar institution would be considered useful. A salary of £50 per annum was offered, with the possibility of it rising to £75 in time.

The successful applicant was Mrs Mary Bedwell. Her time at the prison appears to have passed without incident for nearly ten years, but in 1855, the behaviour of her assistant matron got her into serious trouble.

At the meeting of the Quarter Sessions in March 1855, it was revealed that earlier that year, a female debtor had been brought to the prison by a sheriff's officer from Bristol, at about nine o'clock one evening. The under matron, Miss Wigmore, was on duty that night, and in the presence of this sheriff's officer, the porter and several others, fell down drunk and had to be carried to her apartment. To make matters worse, an 'industrial officer' named Coates was discovered in her apartment (later saying he had gone there to return something he had borrowed).

The matter was only discovered by the Gloucestershire magistrates when they heard something of it from Bristol. It transpired that the matron, along with the governor, the chaplain, the surgeon and the porter, had decided not to report the incident to the Visiting Justices, in order to save Miss Wigmore her job. An investigation had resulted in the under matron being sacked and the matron, Mrs Bedwell, sending in her resignation. The latter was asked to stay in her post for a while, so that she could instruct her successor.

In July 1855, at the Quarter Sessions, a memorial was read out from Mrs Bedwell, 'praying for a retirement pension in consideration of the helpless debility to which she had been reduced by assiduously attending to her duties between nine and ten years in an artificially heated atmosphere, with frequent changes to cold draughts, and being now wholly without resources for the future'. The chairman indicated that he could not recommend that Mrs Bedwell's request be granted, but any magistrate was at liberty to put forward a motion on the subject. Nobody did so and the matter was dropped.

Mary Bedwell's successor as matron was Miss Ellen Gillett, who previously had been deputy superintendent of the female department at Brixton Prison. She stayed at Gloucester until July 1867. Like the previous matron, Miss Gillett left 'under a cloud'. At the October meeting of the Quarter Sessions, she was called upon to give an explanation of 'certain irregularities' at the female prison. She and the under-matron had resigned over questions raised concerning 'the disposal of some articles', and Miss Gillett had faced a charge which was brought against her by the Inspector of Prisons. Magistrate Mr Berwick Baker said that he had always considered Miss Gillett to be a very good officer, but over-attention to her duties and not taking sufficient relaxation meant she had brought herself to a very nervous state.

Mrs Renwick, who succeeded Miss Gillett, served a probationary period before being confirmed in the position at the Quarter Sessions in October 1867. She did not stay at Gloucester for long, however, as she went to Brixton Prison as deputy superintendent in the summer of 1868.

In January 1873, the matron, Miss Mortimer, resigned, after five years' service. She was replaced by Miss Emily Marshall, previously the assistant matron, who stayed at Gloucester until January 1893, when she handed in her resignation. It was reported that she had 'served the county' for twenty-nine years and six months. She got married soon after leaving, and she was awarded a pension of a little over forty pounds.

During the early years of the prison, the matron was the only female employee at Gloucester, but as time went on, more women were brought in to help her and, like the male staff, a hierarchy developed during the nineteenth century within the female part of the prison. The matron was the highest ranking female, being answerable to the governor. Next was the under matron (or assistant matron), and then several female warders.

The hierarchy of roles for female prison staff afforded opportunities for promotion, just as was the case for the male employees. In January 1874, the under-matron, Miss Gee, left Gloucester to take up a position at Lincoln Prison. Her place was taken by Miss Sweetland, the schoolmistress, whose position in turn was taken by her sister, Miss Emily Sweetland.

It was common for female staff to take on other roles in the prison when needed. In January 1853, Gloucester Prison advertised in the *Gloucester Journal* for a 'competent person, between thirty and forty-five, to fill the situation of Hospital Nurse'. Her duties would be to attend on sick female prisoners, and to prepare the food for all hospital prisoners, both male and female. In addition to her main role, she would be asked to assist in the discipline of the prison when required. She would have to reside within the prison. The salary offered was £36 a year.

In January 1868, an advertisement appeared in the *Gloucester Journal* for a female hospital attendant who would also act as schoolmistress, instructing the female prisoners in basic reading, writing and plain needlework. She had to be aged between thirty and forty-five, and she would have to reside in the prison. The salary offered was £40 per annum, with a furnished apartment with fuel and light.

Originally, the matron had been the head laundress at Gloucester, supervising the work of the female prisoners, but later this became a separate role. In February 1871, Mrs Miller retired as head laundry officer. She was presented by the governor on behalf of the officers with a 'very handsome' teapot, cream jug and tray. A less happy departure from the prison befell head laundress Miss Higgs in September 1873, when she died of typhoid fever.

In the Report of the Prison Commissioners published in 1879, only three females were recorded as employees at Gloucester Prison, being the matron and two warders. When the government had taken over the running of the prison in April 1878, there had been five female employees, including a schoolmistress. By 1881, the number of female staff was back up to five, consisting of the matron and four warders. No specific mention was made of a laundry officer, a schoolmistress, or a nurse.

4

TYPES OF PRISONER

Classes of prisoner

Everyone who was admitted to Gloucester Prison was placed in a particular class, depending on the reason for their imprisonment and whether they were male of female. The rules published in 1790 defined the various classes into which the inmates of Gloucester Prison should be divided:

Classes of Prisoner, 1790

Class I. Male felons, divided into
(1) capital or old offenders
(2) petty larceny and young offenders
Class II. Female felons
Class III. King's Evidence
Class IV. Condemned to die
Class V. Male fines
Class VI. Female fines
Class VII. Male debtors
Class VIII. Female debtors
Class IX. Male penitentiary or convicted felons
Class X. Female penitentiary or convicted felons
Class XI. Bridewell

Within the prison buildings, the gaol held the felons, the debtors, the fines, 'King's Evidence' prisoners, and those who had been condemned to death. 'Felons' in prison terminology meant those who were awaiting trial on charges of felony. It was intended that male felons should be divided into two sections, with those charged with the most serious types of felony or who had previous convictions being separated from first offenders or those charged with less serious felonies. Females were not divided in the same way, probably because there were too few of them to be worth doing so.

'King's Evidence' meant felons who had agreed to give evidence against their accomplices, in exchange for not being prosecuted themselves. 'Condemned to die' referred to prisoners who had been sentenced to death at the Assizes. The 1790 rules divided this class into murderers and non-murderers. Murderers suffered harsher treatment, being kept in solitude on bread and water. 'Fines' usually referred to those who were in prison in lieu of paying a fine, or for want of finding sureties for good behaviour.

The penitentiary held those sentenced to terms of imprisonment, with or without hard labour. The 'convicted felons' referred to meant persons whose death sentences had been commuted, and prisoners who were waiting to be transported. The bridewell (house of correction) was for those convicted of misdemeanours at the County Petty Sessions.

In 1808, Sir George Onesiphorus Paul devised new rules for the prison and some changes were made to the classes of prisoners. The house of correction within the prison had closed down by this time, so only prisoners brought in from other houses of correction were classified. The penitentiary prisoners were divided simply into 'Class I, Male Penitentiaries or Convicted Felons' and 'Class II, Female Penitentiaries or Convicted Felons'. The most changes were made to the rules concerning prisoners held in the gaol, with an attempt being made to simplify the descriptions of the classes, but extra sub-divisions being added in the case of the male fines (Class V).

Classes of Prisoner in the Gaol, 1808

Class I. Male felons, divided into

(1) charged with a capital felony or previously convicted of a felony

(2) charged with simple felony and not previously convicted of felony

Class II. Female felons

Class III. Accomplices in felony, admitting evidence for the Crown

Class IV. Prisoners under sentence of death

Class V. Males divided into

(1) charged with misdemeanours and others wanting sureties to appear at Assizes and Quarter Sessions

(2) convicted of misdemeanours in execution of sentence

(3) detained for pecuniary penalties unsatisfied

Class VI. Females charged with and convicted of misdemeanours, or detained for pecuniary penalties unsatisfied

Class VII. Male debtors, prisoners on exchequer process, and for contempt of court

Class VIII. Female debtors or prisoners…, as for males

Class IX. Prisoners brought in from Houses of Correction to appear at Quarter Sessions

Cells on an upper tier in A Wing. (Jill Evans, 2017)

The vast majority of inmates at Gloucester Prison were adult males, who either were waiting to be tried, were serving prison sentences, or were being held in lieu of paying a fine. There were some other categories of prisoner at Gloucester, whose treatment was in some ways different to that of the majority.

Women

For the first 113 years of its existence, Gloucester Prison held both male and female prisoners. When planning the design and operation of the new prison, Sir George Onesiphorus Paul had recognised the need to keep females apart from males as much as possible, but perhaps because there were always far fewer women than men in the prison, very little thought seems to have been given as to how they should be governed.

In the 1790 rules, the same directions were applied to male and female prisoners, except that in the case of female felons, irons should not be used on them 'in ordinary circumstances, regardless of the charge, even if it is murder', and in the penitentiary, officials were to bear in mind 'their sex and ability where given work'.

In 1808, two important new rules were introduced regarding female prisoners. The first was that a salaried matron should be employed, answerable to the governor, who would supervise the work in the laundry and be in charge of the female prisoners. The second was that no male officer was to enter a cell where a female was alone, unless accompanied by the matron.

Both of these rules were no doubt added because of problems during the first years after the prison opened, caused by there being only male officers to deal with female prisoners. For example, in January 1794, the governor recorded in his journal that a turnkey called Hatchett had been found in the lazaretto with Olive Compton, who had just been admitted and was waiting to be examined by the surgeon. Compton complained that Hatchett had taken 'indecent liberties' with her, and told her he would sleep with her that night.

Although women made up a small percentage of prisoners, they were by no means quiet and unassuming. When Paul had a look around the prison on 3 February 1792, he commented in the

Visiting Justices' journal on the unseemly conduct of the female felons. On 5 September 1795, the governor recorded in his journal that the male prisoners were orderly, but the females 'not so much so as could be wished'.

Over the decades, there was a great deal of debate over the types of work which could be given to male prisoners, particularly those sentenced to undergo 'hard labour'. Such debates rarely took place regarding female prisoners, because the main form of work for females at Gloucester throughout the years that women were held there was to do the prison's washing and ironing. This helped to save the county the expense of employing someone to do this essential task, but it caused problems at times when there were only a few female prisoners. In 1808, the governor noted in his journal that there were only two women in the prison, both of whom were unable to work in the laundry, so he had to hire 'two women from the town' to do it.

When Paul gave evidence to the Holford's Committee in 1811, he said that doing the washing was the chief employment of the female convicts. Because the women had to work together in the laundry, 'the rules for solitude be therefore superseded'. This problem was overcome when a new female prison was opened in 1850. A reporter from the *Gloucester Journal* visited the laundry, which was attached to the female prison. He described how the water was heated by steam and conveyed through pipes into separate compartments, where the women worked silently and alone.

The need to have the laundry work done sometimes meant that the education of female prisoners suffered. In November

1846, the Visiting Justices' journal recorded that the matron had complained that during the shorter days of autumn and winter, 'the schooling under Miss Lloyd materially interferes with the business of the laundry'. Because of this, it was ordered that for the first three days of the week, only untried females and those in the penitentiary who were unable to do laundry work would have their schooling.

During the days of the old castle gaol, some women were said to have become pregnant whilst imprisoned. This did not happen in the new prison (as far as is known), but pregnant women were admitted, some of whom gave birth while awaiting trial or undergoing sentence. On 30 March 1792, the surgeon noted in his journal that Ann Daniels, who was pregnant, fainted at the bar during her trial. He sent her to the infirmary, where another prisoner nursed her. On 8 May, Daniels was 'delivered of a female bastard child'. In October 1792, the surgeon recorded that a female felon was working very hard in the laundry, despite being 'big with child'. He ordered her to be given extra food, but on 21 December, her infant was stillborn.

Women sometimes entered the prison bringing their infants with them. In January 1795, a prisoner named Hannah Large was committed on a charge of sheep-stealing. It was recorded in the Visiting Justices' journal that she had with her, 'a child at the breast about eight months old. The infant being in a very filthy state, it appears necessary that it should be cleaned and furnished with proper clothing according to its age, which the Governor is desired to provide.'

The governor consulted with Paul as to what should be done about the child, whose presence was disturbing parts of the prison. Paul said that it must stay with its mother as long as it was being breast fed. This continued to be applied in the case of mothers with infants over the following decades. When new rules were introduced in 1837, it was specified that women coming into prison with a child, or who gave birth while inside, could keep the infant with them, until it had been 'weaned'.

Occasionally the chaplain carried out baptisms of infants who were in the prison with their mothers. In December 1833, the Revd Cooper wrote in his journal that he had baptised the infants of Ann Wilkins and Elizabeth Arnold, who were serving prison sentences in the gaol. The baptisms took place in the chapel, with the prison nurse and a male warder acting as sponsors.

In January 1847, the Visiting Justices called the attention of the Quarter Sessions to the increasing number of females in the prison who had infants with them. There were five children in the prison at that time, aged between a year and two and a half years old, and all able to walk. The magistrates complained that the increase in the number of children incarcerated with their mothers interfered with the discipline and well ordering of the prison. If things continued as they were, they believed it would be necessary to provide a nursery.

In the second half of the 1840s, when the new Separate Prison was built, a new women's prison was constructed using parts of the old gaol and chapel. Magistrates and journalists went to look round the buildings in 1850, but only the *Gloucester Journal* reporter had a look at the grounds of the women's prison: 'It occupies the third range of buildings and is gained by crossing a square yard, entirely enclosed by buildings, and laid out with flowers and borders, divided by paths, in the French fashion of gardening.' At one end of the prison was the laundry, housed in a circular building, in which the women worked.

When the new buildings opened, the government's prison inspector commented that he felt that the amount of accommodation provided for female prisoners was too great. (The number of places was not given at this time, but in 1878 there was room for fifty women.) Thomas Fulljames, the county surveyor and designer of the new buildings, responded that a section of the women's prison had been designed in such a way that it could be given over to male prisoners, if required, without interfering with the privacy of the women.

The numbers of female inmates at Gloucester continued to decline in the second half of the nineteenth century. In 1898, the Annual Report on Gloucester Prison, presented to the Quarter Sessions, revealed that during the preceding year, the daily average number of prisoners had been seventy-four males and only eight females. In 1904, the decision was made to close down the women's prison at Gloucester.

Juveniles

When the prison opened in 1791, it was intended that juveniles should be kept away from the corrupting influence of experienced adult criminals. However, this proved to be impractical, especially in the early years of the prison, when there weren't enough youngsters to warrant them being kept separate from adults. As time went on, however, the number of boys being admitted to the gaol increased.

During 1816, several boys aged between ten and fifteen were in the prison, all of whom had been sentenced to death at the Assizes for theft, then reprieved. In September that year, the chaplain noted in his journal that it would be an important step forward if there was a separate division for boys. He repeated this observation in January 1819.

When Sir George Onesiphorus Paul gave evidence to the committee investigating the state of the gaols in June 1819, he was questioned closely about the treatment of juveniles in the prison. Paul admitted that due to expenses, there was no separate class for juveniles, although there was an increasing number of youths in the prison. At that time, Gloucester held eight or nine boys aged under sixteen.

If possible, Paul said, the boys were put under the supervision of a 'good, steady adult prisoner', but they were not allowed to sleep in the same cells as adults. The boys did not attend any special educational classes, but they were given bibles, prayer books, religious tracts and spelling books. The governor told the committee that the boys used their recreation time to learn spelling on their own, and they also had two or three hours a day with an adult prisoner.

In October 1820, an entry in the Visiting Justices' journal noted that a separate class for boys was very much needed. It wasn't until 1827 that steps finally were taken to achieve this aim; the Seventh Report of the Society for the Improvement of Prison Discipline, published that year, recorded that a separate class for juvenile offenders was to be formed at Gloucester.

Keeping juveniles apart from the adults did not necessarily help to control their behaviour. In June 1832, the chaplain recorded that he had found the juveniles 'noisy and troublesome'. In October of the same year, he reported to the Quarter Sessions that during the previous three months, the most refractory prisoners had been the juvenile felons, 'over whom there has been great difficulty to establish control'.

The problem of controlling youngsters continued into the next decade. At the end of December 1846, one of the magistrates wrote in the Visiting Justices' journal that the juveniles were unruly, and he recommended to the Quarter Sessions 'the expediency of giving corporal punishment with the birch and of finding some employment for them'.

The middle of the nineteenth century saw the development of reformatories for juvenile prisoners. Boys sentenced at the Gloucestershire courts often went to Hardwicke Reformatory, which had been opened by Thomas Berwick Lloyd-Baker in 1852. In his report to the Quarter Sessions in October 1855, the prison chaplain stated that fifteen boys had gone to Hardwicke, and two more to other reformatories. In 1865, it was decided that female juveniles from Gloucestershire should be sent to Red Lodge Reformatory School, in Bristol.

Despite the development of reformatories, the prison continued to be used for children undergoing short sentences, which were usually accompanied by a whipping. The youngest boy known to have been imprisoned at Gloucester was Edgar Kilminster, aged seven. In 1870, he was sentenced with his nine-year-old brother William to seven days' hard labour and twelve strokes of the birch, for stealing sweets. In the same year, four other boys, aged between eight and twelve, served similar sentences for theft. The youngest girl known to have served time in Gloucester Prison was aged twelve.

In the early twentieth century, new legislation was brought in to deal with prisoners aged between sixteen and twenty-one, who were named 'juvenile adults'. Offenders within that age group who were sent to local prisons were kept under the 'Borstal system', which meant they were treated in much the same way as youths who were sent to Borstals.

The Annual Report of the Prison Commissioners, published in October 1906, included information from Gloucester Prison's chaplain, who stated that five juvenile adults had enjoyed the benefits of the Borstal system in operation at Gloucester, so far as was practicable. However, only one of the young men had been there for any length of time, and the chaplain didn't believe the system could work on those sentenced to short terms of imprisonment.

The Borstal Committee for Gloucester Prison released a report in May 1907, in which it was stated that from 1 June 1906 to 31 March 1907, twenty-seven prisoners had been treated under the new rules for juvenile adults. The daily average had been two.

In the Report of the Prison Commissioners published in October 1907, the governor of Gloucester Prison described the treatment of the juvenile adults there. These 'lads' had been kept apart from the other prisoners and 'specially visited' by the chaplain and governor. Also, the Visiting Justices had given them encouragement and advice on their visits.

Addresses had been given to them by the chaplain and his curates, the Visiting Justices, and the governor, on such subjects as Gambling, Duty, Manliness and Honesty. In addition, the young men had undertaken physical training daily, led by a competent instructor. Especial interest had been taken in them after their discharge, and most satisfactory reports had been received as to their conduct, showing that the special treatment in prison had produced good results.

When the Revd Pritchard resigned as prison chaplain in 1939, he addressed the members of the Discharged Prisoners' Aid Society, from which he also had resigned as Honorary Secretary. Recalling his work with young offenders, he said that in 1922, there had been 104 juvenile adults in Gloucester Prison, but he was pleased to say that there had never been that many since.

Debtors

Debtors were people who had been put into prison for failing to pay back money which they owed. Their creditors could apply in the civil courts for those who owed them money to be confined in gaol, until they were paid back. Debtors were not put into prison as a punishment, but to hold them securely, without the possibility of them disappearing without paying back whatever they owed. They were not criminals, and the 1790 rules made it clear that the regulations concerning them were 'intended purely for the preservation of health and morals, decency and good order'.

The rules stated that debtors were to be held in the gaol, where they could have their own 'separate, furnished bedrooms', and could bring in their own bedding and linen if they wished. Debtors could do work provided by the prison and keep one third of their earnings. If they had their own work brought in from outside, they could keep all the money they made. If they had no money and couldn't work, they could get donations from the gaol's charity fund.

Debtors could see visitors between nine in the morning and sunset, every day except Sunday. They were to go to their rooms at nine o'clock in the evening in winter and at ten o'clock in summer. They could buy clothing, food and up to a pint of wine or a quart of beer a day. They could not be punished by being placed in a dark or light cell, nor could they be whipped. In serious cases of indiscipline, they would be sent to the Refractory or Common Ward.

When Sir George Onesiphorus Paul carried out his survey of the prison in 1808, he produced statistics for the number of prisoners held between 1791 and 1807. He calculated that there had been a total of 754 debtors held at Gloucester. The fewest number was in the year 1793, when there were twenty-eight; the greatest was in 1802, when there were sixty-four.

Debtors who could not earn enough money to support themselves could suffer great distress while imprisoned. Creditors who had those who owed them money sent to prison were supposed to pay towards their maintenance, but in practice, this did not always happen. Gloucester Prison held various charity funds from which they could help out destitute prisoners, including one fund specifically for debtors.

The *Gloucester Journal* on 18 July 1796 contained a detailed account of the Charities Fund, from 10 March 1795 to 1 July 1796. The fund for the Relief and Discharge of Poor Debtors listed various donations from private benefactors, plus money put into the charity box outside the gatehouse, totalling a little under £19. Unfortunately, over £40 had been paid out to debtors, but the deficit was made up by transferring money from the general charity fund.

A note stated that from the fund, seven debtors had been 'relieved and discharged', while nineteen others had been 'relieved in distress'. In addition, Mrs Ann Badger of Gloucester had bequeathed £100 to be used to discharge poor debtors from the gaol. To date, nine prisoners had been discharged, using £66. 9s of the bequest.

In 1812, James Neild published *The State of the Prisons in England, Scotland and Wales*. Neild was particularly interested in the imprisonment of debtors, and he gave a detailed description of the conditions for those held in Gloucester Prison, which he visited in November 1802. The debtors, he said, had a spacious airy court, seventy yards in length and nineteen yards wide, with a colonnade at each end. There was a dayroom, with two fire-places, which was 'fitted up with every accommodation for frugal cookery', and two 'large, commodious' workrooms.

There were two wards for debtors. The first was the Magistrates' Ward, to which all debtors were sent when first admitted. Those in this ward were provided with a cell to sleep in, furnished with an iron bedstead, a hair mattress, blankets, sheets and a quilt, all of which was paid for by the county. Anyone who would not abide by the rules of this ward was sent to the Sheriff's Ward, where they had to pay one shilling a week for a bed, or two shillings and six pence if they also needed bedding.

Altogether there were thirty-four single cells provided for male debtors to sleep in. Women debtors had a large room on the first storey of the gaol, containing five beds. In addition, there were two large rooms, holding five beds each, for any times when the number of debtors committed exceeded the number of single cells available. Anyone who could afford it could pay for superior accommodation in 'the Keeper's house'.

In 1808, when the rules were revised at Gloucester, the debtors' accommodation was divided into three sections: the Common Ward, for those with enough means to support themselves without working or receiving county aid; the Ward of Industry, for those without means, who wanted to work to support themselves; and the Irregular Ward, for those who had broken the rules. If a debtor couldn't work enough to sustain himself, he could have the county allowance and two pence per day. Those who could afford it could still pay to be lodged in superior accommodation.

The prison officials found the debtors especially troublesome, probably because they could not use the same punishments on them as on the criminal prisoners. The debtors particularly disliked governor Thomas Cunningham, who was in charge at Gloucester from 1792 to 1836. In February 1793, the surgeon noted in his journal that they had tied a 'scurrilous written paper' against the governor to the collar of a dog.

In January 1808, Cunningham was assaulted by an unruly debtor, who 'struck him a severe blow'. In 1813, debtor James Champion was exhibiting such violent behaviour that when Cunningham had to go and see him after the latest of many incidents, he took a pistol with him.

Debtors who were far more educated than most of their fellow inmates also caused problems for the prison authorities. One such was John Yeates, a solicitor, who was imprisoned as a debtor in November 1808. He wrote a number of letters to the newspapers protesting about his treatment.

Yeates was followed as chief troublemaker by John Perrin, who organised petitions which were sent to the Houses of Parliament. One petition was presented in June 1814 by Lord Stanhope to the House of Lords, in which Perrin complained of 'gross oppression' towards him and his fellow debtors in Gloucester Gaol by Mr Cunningham.

In response, the Lord Chancellor said that he understood Gloucester Gaol to be one of the best regulated in the country, and that Mr Cunningham was highly regarded by the magistrates. The matter was raised on several more occasions by Lord Stanhope.

In 1826, construction began in the prison grounds on a new Debtors' Prison. This freed up space in the gaol, but it caused more disciplinary problems, because some of its windows looked down into the yard of the female felons.

On 29 July 1832, the chaplain wrote in his journal that the debtors had 'induced the females to dress up some kind of image, intended as a reflection on the Governor, and when detected, they encouraged the females by loud vociferations in their disgraceful conduct'.

In March 1833, the chaplain again pointed out the problem of the debtors' apartments overlooking the female felons' yard, which encouraged the women to behave badly. He suggested that it would help if blinds were put up in the windows of the Debtors' Prison. This was done in June, much to the disgust of the debtors.

Complaints by debtors continued after Cunningham's time as governor. In 1843, a petition was presented to the magistrates at the Quarter Sessions, signed by Augustus Newton, who was a barrister by profession, and several other debtors.

Their complaints were: that 'obstructions and inconveniences' were put in the way of them receiving visits from friends and legal advisers, and that they had to converse with visitors through an iron grating, exposed to currents of cold air, and other annoyances 'which would disgrace the dungeons and tortures of the holy inquisition'; that obstructions were placed in their accommodation which excluded light and air and 'shut them out from all sight and knowledge of the external world'; that they didn't have enough space in which to exercise; that they were locked up in 'solitary confinement' too early in the day; that certain debtors were put on the dietary intended for hard labour prisoners; and that they weren't allowed enough coals.

In 1869, a new Debtors' Act came into force, which was intended to end the imprisonment of persons who owed money. In practice, people could still be imprisoned for up to six weeks, if the courts were satisfied that they did have the means to pay their creditors. Debtors continued to be sent to Gloucester Prison, but were fewer in number, and most were held for very short periods.

View of prison buildings from the top of Longsmith Street car park. The structure to the front with the lower roof is the Debtors' Prison. This building originally was three storeys high. (Jill Evans, 2013)

Political Prisoners

When the new county prison opened in 1791, the government soon began to view it as a useful place to send political prisoners, due to its separation of prisoners and use of single cells. Paul strongly objected to the prison being used in this way, but there was nothing he could do to prevent it.

In May 1796, the first political prisoner was committed to Gloucester's penitentiary. Kid Wake was a Gosport book-binder, who had been sentenced to five years' imprisonment with hard labour, for shouting 'No King, No War', at King George III as he drove through London in his carriage, in October 1795. (Wake was referring to British involvement in the war against Revolutionary France.)

Wake spent the whole of his sentence at Gloucester, being released in May 1801. During the first three months of his sentence, he had to stand in the pillory in the middle of Gloucester for four hours, on every market day. In 1799, a poster was printed in London which denounced the 'solitary confinement' in which he was supposedly kept, illustrated with a picture of Wake in his cell, dressed in prison uniform and with an iron ring round his ankle.

During 1799, Kid Wake was joined by three more political prisoners. In May, John Binns was committed to Gloucester, on the orders of the Home Secretary, the Duke of Portland. Binns was a member of the London Corresponding Society and chairman of some of its committees. He had been arrested on a number of occasions before being sent to Gloucester. The governor noted in his journal that he had not received any orders as to what he should do with his new charge, so he would treat him as an untried prisoner.

Binns was followed in August by John Bone and Robert Keir. Bone was a London bookseller who was Secretary of both the London Reforming Society and the London Corresponding Society. Bone and Keir were committed to Gloucester by the Duke of Portland, for committing 'treasonable practices'. The three men proved to be troublesome, frequently complaining about their treatment, sometimes refusing to get out of bed or go to chapel, and fighting each other. The governor and Visiting Justices were relieved when Binns, Bone and Keir were removed from their charge, in March 1801.

John Harriot Hart was sent to Gloucester Prison in July 1808, on the order of the King's Bench Court, to serve a sentence of three years. Hart was the printer and publisher of *The Independent Whig*, and he had been convicted of printing libellous articles against judge Sir Simon Le Blanc and Lord Chief Justice Lord Ellenborough, after William Chapman, the captain of a slave ship, had been tried and acquitted of the murder of two of his crew. Hart was discharged from Gloucester on the completion of his sentence, in July 1811.

In 1817, two political prisoners were held in Gloucester's gaol from April until December. John Bagguley and John Roberts were sent to Gloucester under a warrant from the Right Honourable Viscount Sidmouth, on suspicion of committing high treason, by being part of a plot to attack the banks, courts, prisons and military barracks in Manchester and other cities. The pair were released towards the end of December, after entering into recognizances of £100 to keep the peace.

Just over a hundred years later, eleven leading members of Sinn Fein were imprisoned at Gloucester. Seventy Sinn Fein members had been arrested in Dublin in May 1918, under the terms of the Defence of the Realm Act, and brought to England, where they were allocated to various prisons. One of those sent to Gloucester was Arthur Griffith, who had been Vice-President of Sinn Fein since October 1917. Whilst a prisoner at Gloucester, he was elected as the Member of Parliament for East Cavan, in the 1918 General Election. Several of his fellow prisoners also were elected.

In February 1919, there was an outbreak of influenza in the country; several of the political prisoners at Gloucester became seriously ill and were moved to a nursing home to be cared for. On 6 March, Pierse McCan, the M.P. for Tipperary, died. His fellow Sinn Fein prisoners were released soon afterwards.

5

PRISON LIFE

When prisoners were admitted to Gloucester Prison, they were taken into the gatehouse, where they were searched, had any personal belongings taken off them, and were allocated to a particular class. If deemed necessary, they were given a bath, then they were put into the lazaretto cells, where they were examined by the prison surgeon. If they had no contagious complaints, they were taken to their class, where the rules were read out to them.

Every prisoner slept in an individual cell, containing an iron bedstead, with a straw mattress, a rug, a blanket and a coarse linen or hempen sheet. After 1808, the amount of bedding was increased and consisted of a straw mattress, a hair mattress, two blankets, a rug and two hempen sheets. When the Separate Prison opened in 1850, prisoners slept on hammocks, which could be rolled up during the day, leaving plenty of space in which to work.

The routine for prisoners was much the same every day, except for Sunday. Every morning, the prisoners were woken by a bell, which rang at six o'clock in the summer and at sunrise in winter. The rules stated that prisoners were to get up, make their beds, and wash their faces and hands. The sound of a second bell meant it was time for chapel. After prayers, the governor held roll call, checked the cleanliness of prisoners and distributed bread.

While the prisoners were at prayers, the turnkeys examined the night cells and then locked the stair gates which led to them. During the day, the prisoners carried out their work tasks, if they had any, and spent some time exercising in one of the airing yards. Dinner was in the middle of the day and after another roll call, lock-up was at sunset.

On Sunday, there was no work, but the prisoners had to attend a service at the chapel, where the chaplain would preach a sermon.

The prison chapel, with B Wing to its left, seen from the exercise yard. (Jill Evans, 2013)

Clothing and Hair

According to the 1790 rules, untried prisoners were supposed to wear prison uniform, but this does not seem to have always happened in practice. In January 1792, Paul wrote in the Visiting Justices' journal that some felons were dressed in a mixture of prison uniform and their own clothes, and complained that the rules in this case were unintelligible.

Convicted prisoners who went into the penitentiary had to wear prison uniform. The rules stated that this should be of coarse material and include the wearing of a badge, 'as well to humiliate the wearer as to facilitate discovery in case of escape'. Their own clothes were cleaned and then stored, to be returned to them when they were released. If their own clothing was in too bad a state to be returned to them, they would be provided with replacement items in which to leave the prison.

The rules never specified what exactly the prison uniform should consist of, but an entry in the Visiting Justices' journal on 28 July 1791 described the uniform for men as being white jackets and trousers. By 1799, when an illustration of political prisoner Kid Wake was published, the prison uniform was a blue and yellow patchwork jacket and trousers, plus a cap and wooden-soled shoes.

In 1811, evidence concerning the clothing provided for Gloucester's prisoners was given to the Holford's Committee. Males were supplied with a jacket, a waistcoat, trousers, a flannel shirt, a linen shirt, a night cap, a day cap, two pairs of shoes, and two pairs of stockings. Females were issued with an under petticoat, an upper petticoat, a pair of stays, a linen shift, a flannel shift, a day cap, a night cap, two pairs of shoes, and two pairs of stockings.

When new building works were completed at the prison in 1850, a reporter from the *Gloucester Journal* who visited described the penitentiary prisoners as being 'dressed in motley, one arm, one leg, and one half of the whole man being blue, and the other yellow. We can compare these gaol birds to nothing more apt than goldfinches'.

After the government took over the running of local prisons in 1878, a uniform incorporating broad arrows was introduced for convicted prisoners. This was to make identification easier in the case of escapes and to mark the clothing as being government property. In the first half of the twentieth century, the uniform was a grey jacket and trousers.

The original rules stated that male penitentiary prisoners should have their heads shaved. No particular instructions were given regarding women. In the revised rules of 1808, it was stated that female penitentiary prisoners were not to have their heads shaved. Male penitentiary prisoners should not have their heads shaved for the last six months of their sentence, and not at all if they were serving less than six months.

These changes were intended to make it less easy to identify prisoners as ex-convicts after they left prison. In 1837, the rules were altered again, and it was now stated that 'the hair of every prisoner, male and female, shall be cut as short as possible, and kept so, except in the case of females it shall be allowed to grow for two months before discharge.'

Irons and Fetters

Irons and fetters had been used on all prisoners in the old castle gaol, largely because of the insecure conditions in which they were kept. The 1790 rules for the new prison stated that irons were not be used in ordinary custody on unconvicted males, except for those on a capital charge, or an old offender, or on a prisoner who had tried to escape. Prisoners in the fines section of the gaol were to be fettered only if troublesome. Females were not to be fettered at all.

Male penitentiary prisoners were to wear an iron collar round their necks or a ring round one of their legs. It was not stated whether female penitentiary prisoners wore the same. In the 1808 rules, no mention was made of iron collars or leg rings being worn by penitentiary prisoners of either gender.

Visitors

The monotony of the daily routine could be relieved by a visit from a family member or friend. Inmates of the gaol were permitted to see visitors every day, except Sunday. In the 1808 rules, visiting times for felons and fines were given as three hours in the morning and two hours in the afternoon, with any one visit lasting no more than an hour. Debtors could have visitors between nine o'clock in the morning and sunset. Prisoners who had been condemned to death could have visitors between nine and eleven o'clock in the morning, and between two and four o'clock in the afternoon. Visits to prisoners in the penitentiary could only be arranged by writing to a magistrate for permission.

Visitors to gaol inmates had to talk to them through a large, grated iron gate. In cold weather, a wooden door was shut against the grate, so conversation had to be held through two six-inch holes in the door. In the penitentiary, visitors saw the prisoner through two gratings placed six feet apart, with a prison warder sat to one side in between the gratings, listening and observing.

Diet

The 1790 rules stated that inmates of the gaol should be given a daily allowance of bread and money (the 'county allowance'). Men were to receive one and a half pounds of 'good household bread' a day, and one penny to purchase meat, vegetables, etc. Women were to have one pound and three ounces of bread a day, plus a penny. A sutler should be employed who would bring goods to sell, or failing that a messenger, to fetch purchases for prisoners. No alcohol was allowed for criminal prisoners; permitted drinks other than water were milk, buttermilk and tea. Debtors could buy up to a pint of wine or a quart of beer per day.

Prisoners in the penitentiary were to receive one and a half pounds of bread a day, plus twice a week they were to have a pint of strong soup made from coarse, wholesome meat, peas or other vegetables. Prisoners who were working were to be given extra. Penitentiary inmates were not permitted to purchase food for themselves.

In 1808, some changes were made to the dietary. In addition to every prisoner on the county allowance being given one and a half pounds of bread and one penny per day, they also were to be given coal to cook any victuals they purchased themselves. Coffee was added to the list of permitted drinks.

The 1808 rules for the penitentiary prisoners included a detailed dietary plan. It was now specified that convicts, in addition to their daily bread allowance, should have gruel for breakfast, made from one and a half ounces of oatmeal and a quarter ounce of salt, with leeks or other vegetables. The dinner menu varied according to the day of the week:

Sundays and Thursdays - twelve ounces of beef without bone, with one pound of potatoes or other vegetables.

Mondays and Fridays - three quarters of a pint of peas made into soup with broth made from the beef of the preceding day, seasoned with pepper or ginger.

Tuesdays - two pounds of vegetables or a quarter pound of cheese.

Wednesdays - one and a half ounces of rice, one and a half ounces of oatmeal and a quarter ounce of salt, made into gruel, with pepper and ginger.

Saturdays - a quarter of a pound of cheese.

In 1819, when Paul gave evidence to the Select Committee investigating the gaols, he stated that prisoners before trial received bread which was usually two days old. After conviction, they received the same amount of bread as before, plus gruel made of oatmeal and salt, with leeks, onions, or whatever was available from the prison garden. The daily menus for dinner had remained the same as in 1808. He added that females were allowed an ounce of tea and two ounces of sugar instead of gruel.

When the Report of the Select Committee of 1819 was published, the dietary at Gloucester was criticised for being far too liberal, especially with regard to the provision of meat. The penitentiary diet subsequently was reduced to one and a half pints of pea soup on two days a week, and on the other days, one pound of potatoes.

The food provision for Gloucestershire's prisoners came in for regular criticism from the county magistrates. A particular concern was that the food in the prison was better than that in the workhouses, and that paupers were deliberately committing crimes in order to be sent to prison. In 1834, a committee of magistrates investigated the dietaries in the prison and the county's workhouses and compared them. It concluded that the diet in the prison was better than in the workhouses. It was recommended that to address this issue, solid ingredients should be replaced by liquid or pulpy food such as oatmeal or soup, and the amount of food given to prisoners should be reduced. The prison surgeon, Mr Wilton, consented to the changes.

In 1835, a new Act of Parliament came into force which ordered that all rules and regulations made in local prisons, including those concerning the dietary, should be submitted to the government for approval. It was declared as 'most desirable' that convicted prisoners should not be permitted to receive anything more than the jail allowance, but if the prison surgeon believed that extra food was necessary for an individual, he should state the cause and detail the amount given in his journal.

At the meeting of the Quarter Sessions in July 1843, Mr Hickes, the prison surgeon, was summoned to answer questions concerning 'certain entries in the prison journals, from which it appeared that a more liberal scale of dietary had been adopted in the penitentiary', on his orders. Hickes stated that there had been an alarming increase of illness among the penitentiary prisoners, so he had ordered an alteration in the dietary, which had resulted in the health of the prisoners improving. The chairman explained that the surgeon had no authority to do this; he could only change the dietary in individual cases.

Later in 1843, the government came up with a new dietary, which it recommended for local prisons. Its main ingredients were bread, gruel, potatoes, meat, soup and cocoa. Prisoners were divided into classes, depending on the length of their sentences and whether or not they were doing hard labour. The amount and types of food they were given depended on which class they were in.

Number One diet consisted of bread and gruel only, and was the least amount of food that a prisoner could receive. It was given to those serving terms of imprisonment without hard labour, for the first seven days of their sentence. At the other end of the scale, those prisoners who were serving the longest terms of imprisonment, with hard labour, were given all of the six key ingredients, and a much larger ration of potatoes. This was the only class to be given cocoa, which was considered to be beneficial because of its 'oily element'. The beverage served up to prisoners was supposed to be made up of three quarters of an ounce of cocoa of 'solid flake', flavoured with two ounces of milk and six drachms of molasses.

Gloucester Prison introduced this dietary in January 1844, and the surgeon was quick to complain to the Quarter Sessions about it. The daily allowance of bread had been reduced from twenty-four ounces a day to eighteen, and Hickes did not believe that this was enough, especially for prisoners on hard labour. For breakfast, prisoners were allowed only six ounces of bread, and by eleven o'clock, they were complaining of weakness and a disagreeable feeling in the pit of the stomach. Hickes also complained about the cocoa, which was being made without any milk and sweetened with treacle, meaning the prisoners could not stomach it.

The chairman said that the problem with the cocoa was the fault of the cooks, who were serving it up so thick that it acted as an emetic. A magistrate asked if the bread allowance could be put back to twenty-four ounces, but the chairman replied that the court had no power to do this.

The debate over whether inmates of local prisons were being given too much or too little food continued over the following years. In 1864, after a government inquiry into local prison dietaries, it was recommended that meat should only be given to prisoners as an ingredient in soup, and suet pudding was introduced as a substitute for meat.

In 1872, Gloucester Prison carried out an experiment in which canned Australian meat was given to inmates, as a cost-saving exercise. This was tried for a month, then the results were reported to the Quarter Sessions. It was found that there had been very little saving at Gloucester, because the prison had a good deal on fresh meat with a local contractor.

By March of the following year, the price of local meat had risen, so the Gloucestershire magistrates decided to try out Australian meat again. This time, it was found that savings were made, and the meat did not seem to have any adverse effects on the health of the prisoners. Australian canned meat continued to be used in Gloucester Prison for several years. It was only given to prisoners serving terms of six months or more, as part of their dinner menu, two times a week.

In the twentieth century, very little was said in the reports of the Visiting Justices to the Quarter Sessions concerning the prison diet, other than it was 'satisfactory'. When William Sparrow was interviewed by the *Cheltenham Chronicle* in September 1906, on his release from Gloucester Prison after serving two months, he commented that the prison diet was 'sufficient and wholesome, but rough'. For breakfast and supper, he had received a pint of gruel and eight ounces of bread. For dinner, there was meat on Thursdays and Sundays, on two other days there was soup, and on the remaining days there was suet pudding and potatoes.

One meal which attracted the attention of the local press was the dinner given on Christmas Day in 1929, when *The Citizen* reported that plum duff was to be served to prisoners, made of currants, minced apples, raisins and breadcrumbs. The inmates also were to receive extra allowances of roast beef and bread.

Work

The necessity of giving prisoners work and discouraging idleness was an integral part of the reform system introduced at Gloucester Prison. Because of this, it was considered very important that a taskmaster should be employed, to provide work for prisoners and sell any goods made.

An example of the type of work done at the prison was shown in an advertisement which appeared in the *Gloucester Journal* on 3 February 1794. Under the heading 'Gloucester County Gaol', it announced that 'Warm Slippers, made by the Penitentiary Prisoners (for W. Green, Manufacturer)' were on sale at his house in Upper Quay Lane, and at the manufacturing room in the prison.

Prisoners who were being held in the gaol while waiting to be tried could not be forced to work, but if they were receiving the county allowance (bread and a little money every day), they were encouraged to do some sort of labour, unless they were unfit. Profits from any goods made were divided into four parts, with two going to the prisoner, one to the governor and one to the county. Prisoners who agreed to give up the county allowance could have three parts of the profits instead of two.

Penitentiary prisoners had no choice but to work, unless they were incapable of doing so. Those sentenced to hard labour worked for between eight and ten hours a day, depending on the time of year. Hard labour, according to the 1790 rules, was supposed to be 'of the hardest and most servile kind, in which drudgery is chiefly required and where the work is little liable to be spoilt by ignorance, neglect or obstinacy'. Suggested means of hard labour included working on a treadwheel, sawing stone, polishing marble, and beating hemp.

Prisoners not doing hard labour might pick oakum, weave sacks, spin yarn or knit nets. Female penitentiary prisoners were to be given work 'suitable to their sex and ability'. At Gloucester, most women worked in the laundry or did sewing and mending.

In January 1809, Paul told the Quarter Sessions that on one day when he inspected the prison, there had been nine male felons and one female in the gaol. One male was the constable of his division (meaning he was responsible for the sweeping of cells and other chores), and the other eight men were idle. The woman was picking wool.

In the fines division, there were six men and three women. Of the men, one was a cook, one a gardener, one a constable of his division, and the other three were idle. Of the women, two were weaving slippers and one was idle. There were nineteen debtors, of whom seven were working; three were constables of their divisions, three were doing work they had provided for themselves, and one was making nets.

In the penitentiary, most of the sixteen male convicts were employed. Three were weaving sacks, while another was sewing the sacks up. Two were knitting bottle stands, one was doing carpentry, two were weaving stockings, another was weaving a girth web, one was carding wool, one making mops and another was making gloves. Two men were sick and one was 'lame'. Of four female convicts, two were working in the laundry and the other two were making slippers.

In 1811, when Paul gave evidence to the Holford's Committee, he talked about the types of work carried out by prisoners at Gloucester. For those who had been sentenced to hard labour, he said, it had been difficult to find the kinds of work originally suggested as being suitable for male prisoners. This was largely due to the increased use of machinery in industry, which had meant there was little manual work available for prisoners to carry out.

Paul suggested that while work was supposed to intensify the punishment of the prisoner, at Gloucester it was used rather 'to introduce variety to the occupations, to teach trades, and to relieve the mind from that burden which solitude without any object would occasion'.

Providing hard labour for the female convicts was little trouble, Paul said, as they worked in the laundry, unless they were not fit enough to do so. There were a few solitary work-rooms for women who were not employed in the laundry, which were on the first floor of the penitentiary.

Although hard manual labour was difficult to find for male penitentiary prisoners, Gloucester did have a small treadwheel, which pumped water into a storage tank. In 1819, when Paul gave evidence to the Select Committee investigating the gaols, he was questioned further about this water-wheel. He described how four men would go into the yard at a time. Two would exercise while the other two spent five minutes on the wheel. The two teams would alternate over twenty minutes, before being replaced by a new set of four men. All the male convicts took a turn on the wheel, unless they were too old, infirm, or ill.

Governor Thomas Cunningham also gave evidence to the Select Committee. He listed work done by convicts as making stockings and garters, weaving, and making purses and netting. He said that all convicts were made to work, even if it was only picking wool. As for prisoners awaiting trial, Cunningham said that the male felons were not given any work, because of the many escape attempts that had been made using manufacturing materials or tools. It wasn't even possible to give them a loom to weave on, because a knife was needed to cut thread ends, which might be used as a weapon. Female felons made cloth shoes, shirts and seamen's stockings.

In late 1822, a dramatic change came for male penitentiary prisoners undergoing hard labour, with the introduction of a treadwheel. Unlike the water-wheel previously in operation at Gloucester, this machine could accommodate a large number of prisoners at one time. A treadwheel was installed in the penitentiary yard of Gloucester Prison towards the end of December 1822. In January 1823, reporters from the local newspapers were invited to see the new apparatus in operation.

The *Gloucester Journal* said that at the time of their reporter's visit, there were thirty-six men on the wheel, eighteen on either side. Every two minutes, two men stepped off the wheel and were replaced by two others. Strict discipline was enforced and officers were placed on either side to prevent any talking or 'indecorous behaviour'. While some prisons were installing treadwheels without using them for any purpose, the one at Gloucester was used to grind corn to make flour, and also to bruise barley and pump water.

New rules were introduced at Gloucester in 1837, which stated that work for male penitentiary prisoners was to be 'the tread-wheel only'. Females in the penitentiary were to do the washing or 'other necessary employment of the prison', or if not fit enough to do anything else, they should pick oakum.

In 1850, when the new Separate Prison block was opened, a *Gloucester Journal* reporter who accompanied magistrates on a tour of Gloucester Prison described the working of the treadwheel, which was in operation in the penitentiary yard:

Whilst some were clinging by their hands working on the wheel, others were collected in the yard, walking in a weary round to escape catching cold, and to stretch their legs. Every now and then as the wheel revolved, a whitened step appeared, and then one of the workers would drop down, and one of the walkers would get up, and so the wheel and the punishment was kept moving. Not a word was spoken at the wheel, or off it, nor was it necessary; for each prisoner knew the moment that his spell ceased, so accurately, that he whose turn had come, had no opportunity of forgetting it. One could not fail to be struck by the air of languor, and almost misery, which always marks labour not lightened by reward.

In the Separate Prison, inmates were working on a variety of tasks, either alone or in small groups. The *Gloucester Journal* reporter described different types of work being carried out there. On one tier, he said, were those employed in weaving, on another were shoemakers, etc, etc. Trade instructors, who supervised the prisoners, had rooms within each wing.

In October 1853, the annual report of the Inspector of Prisons for the Southern and Western District was published. At the time of his visit to Gloucester, the inspector had found the 'criminal prisoners' in the Separate Prison engaged in a variety of occupations.

Eighteen inmates were weaving cloth and mat-making. The types of cloth being produced were sacking, tarpaulin, woollen cloth for prisoners' clothing, linen for shirts for the lunatic asylum, linen sheeting, bed-casing and towelling. Mats were made of coconut fibre, some with woollen borders. There were nine looms for weaving cloth and one for mats. Twelve men were engaged in shoe-making. The coarser shoes were for prison use, but some were good enough to be bought by the shops. Of those not engaged in trades, twenty-three men were picking oakum, five were cleaning the prison and two were whitewashing it. Away from the Separate Prison, fifty men sentenced to 'first class hard labour' were working on the treadwheel in the penitentiary yard. Female prisoners were occupied in washing, needlework, knitting, and cleaning the prison.

By the end of the nineteenth century, the treadwheel had fallen out of favour, and its use as a means of hard labour in prisons was abolished by the government. Gloucester removed its treadwheel in 1902, and on its former site a new room was constructed, in which prisoners could work in association with others.

In December 1903, the prison governor stated in his annual report that following the removal of the treadwheel, male prisoners had been found employment making mail bags for the General Post Office and sacks and hammocks for the Admiralty, as well as chopping wood for the War Department, and working in the service of the prison (whitewashing, cleaning, etc). Females continued to do the laundry and mend clothes for prisoners.

In 1943, prisoners were allowed to help in the war effort by going outside to work on the land. In June, the Prison Visiting Committee reported to the Quarter Sessions that thirty prisoners, divided into two parties, were leaving Gloucester Prison every day except Sundays, to carry out agricultural labour in Gloucestershire and Worcestershire, under the War Agricultural Executive Committee's scheme. At that time, they were engaged in drainage work, and an official had said that the prisoners 'worked very well indeed'.

Working outside in parties continued after the war. In September 1949, thirty prisoners were helping in road maintenance work in Stroud and Gloucester, where there was said to be an acute shortage of labour. The men were taken to their workplaces in council lorries; the prison authorities paid their wages. *The Citizen* on 21 September reported that prisoners were working on Bristol Road, between Hardwicke and Gloucester, and were said to 'like it very much'.

Education

Some basic education was given to inmates in Gloucester Prison in the early years, under the supervision of the prison chaplain. He would provide religious books and papers, and spelling books, to prisoners. When Sir George Onesiphorus Paul gave evidence to the Holford's Committee in 1811, he revealed that the chaplain, the Revd Jones, did not encourage prisoners to learn to write or to do basic mathematics, because these were 'unnecessary for their reformation'. The chaplain did believe that it was good for prisoners to be able to read, so they could study the bible and other religious works.

Education was first formally introduced into prisons by the Gaols Act of 1823, which stipulated that basic reading and writing should be taught to prisoners. In 1865, a Prison Act was passed, which stated that prisons must offer instruction in reading and writing and basic arithmetic, but this must not interfere with the time spent doing work tasks. Gloucester Prison was employing school teachers by the middle of the nineteenth century.

In 1853, after an annual visit from the government's Inspector of Prisons, it was reported that at Gloucester Prison, the chaplain would gather all the prisoners in the chapel after daily service and divide them into four classes. He then spent the next two hours teaching each class in succession, instructing them on religious subjects and examining them on the catechism.

The schoolmaster and schoolmistress were under the direction of the chaplain. They taught for five to six hours every day, except Saturday afternoons and Sundays. The chaplain would visit the classrooms to examine the proficiency of prisoners and promote them to other classes, when appropriate.

In September 1897, the report of the Commissioners of Prisons was published, which contained some information on the education system then in practice at Gloucester. The chaplain had reported that during the past year, fifteen prisoners had been under educational instruction, of whom two had 'passed out' of school during their prison term, and five had passed 'the third standard' on their discharge. The remaining eight had not done quite so well, with one of them being 'incapable of instruction'.

After the First World War, prisons increasingly were encouraged by the government to offer a variety of classes for prisoners, with the help of volunteer teachers. In February 1924, the *Gloucester Journal* reported that the governor had been successful in getting the voluntary help of two local gentlemen in 'carrying out the educational reform scheme in prisons, lately introduced by the Prison Commissioners'.

Mr Gladstone Butler, a Fellow of the Certified Teachers of Shorthand, who was an instructor under the Gloucester Education Committee and taught at the technical schools, had started a shorthand class at the prison on the previous Saturday evening, and it was hoped that several inmates would qualify for their certificates. In addition, Mr F.C. Beynon of the Crypt School had started a class in elementary science on Thursdays, which he had promised to continue as long as he was in Gloucester. Classes in French were later added to the curriculum, and in June 1931, the report of the Prison Commissioners stated that an additional elementary class in 'handicraft' (which in this context meant small household repairs) had started too.

In addition to the classes which were introduced into the prison over time, the provision of books was increasingly considered as important. The chaplain always had been able to supply religious reading matter to prisoners, and when the time came that the prison had enough books to keep a small library, he was in charge of that.

When the progressive stage system was introduced into local prisons in the late 1870s, the ability to borrow a library book was one of the 'perks' offered to prisoners on entering a more lenient stage of their sentence. William Sparrow, who served two months in Gloucester in 1906, was largely unimpressed with the books available. During the first stage of his sentence, he only had books given to him by the chaplain, which were all 'of a goody-goody character'. In the library, though, there was a better choice of material, including volumes of *The Quiver* periodical and novels such as *Jane Eyre*.

An innovative way of obtaining more books for the prison was found in May 1947, when the Salvation Army Band held a concert at the Guildhall. Instead of paying an entry fee, the audience was asked to bring gifts of books for the prison library.

Entertainment

The notion of providing entertainment for prisoners would have seemed very strange to eighteenth century reformers like John Howard and Sir George Onesiphorus Paul. In their time, the most a prisoner might look forward to was a good sing-along to the hymns at Sunday's chapel service, and the occasional sermon from a guest preacher in place of the prison chaplain.

There was no radical change to this situation until the twentieth century, when concerts, lectures and plays gradually were introduced into the prison. In October 1911, the chaplain reported to the Prison Commissioners that the 'Civic Quartet', made up of the former mayor and the current city High Sheriff, plus their wives, had visited the prison twice and performed sacred songs and hymns, 'to the great delight of the prisoners'.

In February 1922, *The Citizen* reported that Gloucester Prison had been selected as the scene of a 'pioneer movement in the furtherance of modern ideas for still further humanising and ameliorating the lives of prisoners, with a view to their reformation and conversion into good citizens'. From time to time, lectures and addresses had been given in the prison chapel, but now, the governor had been given permission by the Prison Commissioners to have a theatre company perform a play. The Cotswold Players had agreed to do a production of Jerome K Jerome's *The Passing of the Third Floor Back*. This was 'a humorous piece with a powerful moral lesson underlying it'.

A stage was erected in one of the large corridors of the prison, which had cells running down either side. The prisoners were sat on benches, with a warder at each end. *The Citizen*'s reporter, who had attended the prison before on the occasion of executions, remarked on how strange it was to hear roars of laughter reverberating around the building.

During 1925, a great variety of entertainments took place at the prison. One Saturday in February, the Moody Manners Opera Company put on a show entitled 'Melodies Old and New'.

In September, Mr W.E. Jack gave a lecture on 'Bird Life', in which he spoke chiefly about bird migration. Also in September, the Salvation Army Band visited on a Sunday afternoon and delivered a good programme of music and songs. The Salvation Army Band made regular visits to the prison, as did members of the choir from St Mary de Lode Parish Church.

Punishment

The first rules drawn up for the prison in 1790 detailed the types of punishment which could be applied to misbehaving prisoners. The usual method of punishment was for the troublemaker to be put into some sort of solitary confinement.

Under the heading, 'Scale of Solitary and other Punishments to be applied', the different degrees of punishment were described. The most severe form of solitude was to be placed in a 'dark cell', which had no light, either natural or artificial. The next level down was confinement in a 'light cell', which did have light. The third degree was for the prisoner to be kept in his or her own cell, but allowed to go out alone for air and exercise, and to go to chapel on Sunday. The fourth degree was as the third, except prisoners could associate with others in their class when attending chapel or taking exercise.

The rules gave more details of the punishments which could be used on different types of prisoners. Untried felons, if 'troublesome', could be placed in dark cells, or they could be put in fetters or handcuffs. The chaplain could endorse such punishment to last up to six days. If the prisoner was still disobedient, the governor could apply to a Visiting Justice for 'heavier irons, etc'.

With regard to penitentiary prisoners, the governor could order three days' solitary confinement without having to gain the chaplain's consent. He needed the approval of the chaplain to extend the punishment to six days. The governor could apply to the magistrates for permission to put a prisoner in solitude on bread and water for a month. Visiting Justices could also approve the whipping of the most badly behaved prisoners.

'Troublesome' was defined as refusing to obey, striking or threatening an official, cursing, swearing or being disrespectful to the chaplain, bad behaviour in chapel, committing assault, being abusive, gambling or defrauding another prisoner, passing a boundary fence, attempting to escape, and wasting or damaging goods.

When the prison rules were amended in 1808, the regulations concerning punishment remained much the same, except that in the case of the felons, the governor was now given the power to withhold the money given as part of the county allowance as an alternative punishment to solitary confinement or irons. As for penitentiary prisoners, the only amendment was that it was now specified that females must never be whipped.

The prison staff seem to have put up with a great deal of bad behaviour before they would ask the magistrates to order a whipping for a prisoner. Penitentiary prisoner Joseph Clarke had been put into the dark cells on a number of occasions for insubordination to the governor and unruly conduct, before he was whipped on 11 May 1815. The cause of his punishment was challenging the warders to a fight and having to be carried forcibly to his cell, while he shouted 'Murder!'.

A series of entries in the governor's journal between October and December 1822 shows the types of punishments which were regularly meted out to prisoners, and the kinds of bad behaviour which got them into trouble. All of the punishments given out during this time consisted of some degree of solitary confinement. On 1 October 1822, one male was put in 'Solitude, Dark Cell', for 'answering improperly in Chapel', two women were put in 'Solitude, light cells', for cursing, swearing and abusing each other, and another female was put in a dark cell for the same offence. On 5 October, two male felons were put in the dark cells for gambling. On 8 December, a female prisoner was put in a dark cell for 'making a great noise in the night'. Four other women received the same punishment for a similar offence on 26 December.

New rules were brought in at the prison in 1837, in which the chief means of punishment continued to be solitary confinement. Offenders could be kept in solitary, on bread and water only, for up to three days. Punishment for more serious offences should be decided by the Visiting Justices, who could order close confinement for up to a month, or 'personal correction' in the case of male prisoners convicted of felony or sentenced to hard labour.

In the case of repeat offenders or very bad offences, the Visiting Justices could order punishment either by moderate or repeated whipping. This was to be inflicted with a cat-o'-nine-tails, at a rate of fifteen blows per minute. The degree of whipping was to depend on the age and physical fitness of the prisoner, but was never to be used on females. A cat-o'-nine-tails was to be kept in the prison, which should have a handle three quarters of an inch thick, with the lashes made of 'common three-twist bag twine, used dry'.

In 1877, an inquiry took place to discover how many instances of corporal punishment had taking place in all the country's local prisons, between 14 April 1874 and 31 July 1876. The *Gloucester Journal* reported that in Gloucester Prison, there had been sixty-seven instances, but only one case of the cat-o'-nine-tails being used, ordered by the Visiting Justices on a prisoner for assaulting an officer and refusing to work. Twelve lashes had been administered on that occasion. In all the other cases, the birch was used; most had been ordered by the courts of Petty Sessions as part of a prisoner's sentence, rather than being inflicted for bad behaviour in the prison.

In November 1881, the Report of the Prison Commissioners for the year up to 31 March 1881 was published. At Gloucester Prison, the most common punishment by then was either to be put on a restricted diet, to lose a privilege previously earned, or, in the case of those who were undergoing the progressive stage system of imprisonment, to be put back a stage. The total number of prisoners punished had been sixty-nine men and eighteen women. Going into the twentieth century, loss of privileges continued to be the most common means of punishment.

Illness and Death

In the days of the old castle gaol, diseases such as gaol fever had been rife, sometimes causing the deaths of prisoners before they could even be tried. At the new prison, a requirement that incoming prisoners should be kept in the gatehouse until they had been examined by the surgeon and declared free of any infections had been written into the rules in 1790, to help prevent the spread of anything contagious among the inmates.

Despite this precaution, at times when there were epidemics of infectious diseases in Gloucester, some prisoners usually became ill. In addition, the wells in the prison sometimes became contaminated, especially when the River Severn flooded, which resulted in complaints of diarrhoea among the prisoners, and an occasional case of typhus.

In the surgeon's report to the Epiphany Quarter Sessions in January 1847, he said that there had been a great increase in sickness in the prison during the past quarter, with cases of influenza, cough, diarrhoea, fever, etc, but although the illnesses had been severe, no fatal case had occurred. He added that fever had been prevalent in the city and neighbourhood and many deaths had taken place, but in the prison, every case had recovered. The outcome was not so positive in June 1849, when there was a cholera epidemic in the city. On this occasion, thirteen prisoners became ill, of whom four died.

Moving on to February 1896, when smallpox was rife in Gloucester, there was only one case in the prison. The staff had all been vaccinated previously, but as a precaution, the Prison

Commissioners advised that all the officers should be re-vaccinated.

There always were individual cases of illness in the prison, and as part of his duties, the surgeon attended sick prisoners and administered medicines as required. He could order prisoners to be kept in bed or sent to the infirmary, to be given more clothing or bedding if they were suffering from the cold, and to be allowed extra food.

Sometimes a prisoner died in the prison due to illness, and then a coroner's inquest had to be held. An example of a typical inquest at the prison occurred in 1859, when a female inmate, Caroline Moule, died. She was about eighteen years old, and had been sentenced to eight months' hard labour at the previous Quarter Sessions, for committing a felony. She had been in good health when she entered the prison, but subsequently complained that she had taken cold due to being placed in the dark cell for insubordination towards the laundress, and also that she was unable to eat her food.

The surgeon ordered a change of diet for her, and later had her placed in the prison infirmary, but she died. At the time she went into the infirmary she was suffering from scurvy, which, the surgeon believed, brought on exhaustion, causing death. The inquest jury's verdict was that she died of natural causes.

On 1 November 1894, a prisoner who was working on the treadwheel fell down dead. Henry Johnson, aged forty-five, had been undergoing a term of fourteen days' imprisonment with hard labour, for a theft. The medical officer, Dr Clark, said he had found Johnson to be fit and healthy when he entered the prison on 22 October. He had made no complaint about working on the wheel until a few days before his death, when he had mentioned a feeling of compression in his chest and said that he was suffering from flatulence. Clark had examined him carefully but could find nothing wrong. A verdict was returned that Johnson had died of syncope, which could have happened when he was walking across a road, so was not caused by working on the treadwheel.

As well as dealing with cases of physical sickness, the surgeon had to cope with a significant number of prisoners showing symptoms of mental illness. In most cases, the surgeon, along with the chaplain, the governor and the Visiting Justices, tended to assume that such prisoners were 'feigning insanity'.

The favoured method of assessment was to subject the prisoner to a number of 'treatments' in the hope that this would force them to confess that they were faking. These included dunking the prisoner in a cold bath and applying electric shock treatment. The latter was tried in 1813 on Martha Jeynes, who was having fits. This had a good effect the first time it was used, with Jeynes promising to behave better in future, but further treatments did not work, so the surgeon ordered the turnkey to 'drench her with beer caudle'.

In some cases, the mental instability of a prisoner was beyond doubt. On 10 August 1809, the surgeon reported that the 'Strait Waistcoat' had been used on a male prisoner, described as 'Reed the lunatic'.

In 1837, when new rules were published for Gloucester Prison, it was added to the duties of the surgeon that he should 'enquire into the mental as well as the bodily state of every offender confined by sentence or order in the Penitentiary House, and of every other prisoner who may be under temporary confinement for refractory behaviour'. This new rule was due to a growing concern that solitary confinement, either as part of a prison sentence or as a punishment for bad behaviour while in prison, might be causing or contributing to mental illness.

Unfortunately, a number of inmates ended their own lives whilst being held in the prison. The first such case in the new prison occurred after William Birt had been sentenced to death at the Summer Assizes in 1791. He was due to be executed on the gatehouse roof on 15 August, but he hanged himself in his cell, two days earlier.

In April 1829, after being sentenced to seven years' transportation at the Assizes, Ann Hamerton returned to the prison and hanged herself. At the subsequent coroner's inquest, a verdict was returned of 'Lunacy'.

Henry Simmonds took his own life on 5 October 1884. He was twenty years old and was serving a sentence of eighteen months' imprisonment with hard labour. He ate his breakfast in his cell that morning, but he didn't appear when he was called to exercise a couple of hours later. He was found in his cell, suspended by his bed sheet from an iron bar in the ventilator.

At the County Quarter Sessions in January 1936, Ronald George Carpenter was called into court, to answer charges of shop-breaking and theft. The prison governor had to inform the magistrates that Carpenter was dead, having been found hanging in his cell.

The inner gates of the gatehouse. (Jill Evans, 2013)

6

ESCAPES

When the first prisoners moved into the new prison, all the building work had not yet finished. The carelessness of construction workers in leaving ladders unattended resulted in the first escape taking place on 22 October 1791. A male felon, who had been employed at sawing wood in one of the work rooms, climbed over the boundary wall, using a ladder which builders had left in the yard.

Another escape occurred in that same month, when convict John Cull was sent to collect a ladder and take it to the entrance lodge. He used the ladder to get over the wall, and a rope he had found to lower himself down the other side. His freedom did not last long, as his wife brought him back to the prison the next day.

On the night of 20 July 1792, prisoners Samuel Dent, Daniel Evans and John Stibbs escaped, after a great deal of careful preparation. Stibbs made a hole through the wooden door of his cell, using a gimlet he had managed to get hold of, then was able to unlock the bolt on the outside of the door. After this, there was an iron door to unlock, which he did using a false wooden key which the prisoners had made from manufacturing materials. He then opened the cell doors of the other two men.

They all got down into the yard and through an iron gate, which had been left unlocked, then used a rope which they had made from bits of cord stolen from the manufactory to scale the wall. They had even filled their night caps with sand, which they attached to their rope to act as weights when they threw it over the wall and climbed over. Unfortunately for them, they were back in prison by the beginning of August.

After this escape, the height of the wall was raised and a chevaux de frise was put along its top. A night watchman was employed from then on, and in the manufactory, cordage was no longer made and wood was not used as a work material.

When felon Charles Buckingham escaped in December 1808, the governor suspected that the prison night watchman must have helped him to do it. He also blamed the porter, James Cope, for his carelessness in leaving a mop and some brushes in the yard, which aided Buckingham's escape. The watchman, John Brown, was arrested and tried at the next Assizes for aiding an escape, but he was found not guilty.

About six months after his escape, Buckingham was recaptured in London and the governor escorted him back to Gloucester. He gave an account to the chaplain and the Visiting Justices of how he had got out of the prison, which they did not completely believe. He said after spending a month chiselling at a bar of his cell window, using a knife at first and then a large nail, he had acquired a metal spoon from a turnkey, which he had been able to use as a key to open his cell door.

He left his cell when it was dark, and it took him forty-five minutes to get into the debtors' yard, using cut-up blankets to lower himself down. He had then tied some mops to his sheets and had thrown them over the boundary wall, then climbed over.

When questioned about Buckingham's statement, all of the turnkeys denied giving him a spoon.

At his trial in August 1809, Buckingham was sentenced to death for highway robbery, but this was commuted to transportation for life. On his way to the hulks with three other prisoners, chained together, handcuffed and guarded by three turnkeys, he and two other men escaped from their carriage during a stop for a change of horses. Buckingham was never recaptured.

In 1817, it was discovered that several prisoners had been attempting to make keys, by melting down lead pipes in their cups. A search was made of the cells, on the grounds that a pipe had gone missing, and an L-shaped piece of lead was discovered. One prisoner said that they had been trying to make a mould by baking gravel in the oven, without success; another said they had used a lump of coal to make a mould. All the culprits were put into solitary confinement.

In April 1869, a prison officer was attacked during an escape attempt. At the recent Assizes, Charles Wiltshire had been condemned to death for murdering a woman he found drunk and incapable in the road, and was due to be executed at Gloucester. Instead of being put into a condemned cell, he was placed in a room in the prison infirmary, where he was kept company day and night by two warders who took it in turns to watch over him.

One night, he got behind the guard on duty and hit him on the head with a candlestick, then ran out of the room. The injured warder was able to alert the night watchman, who was passing nearby, and Wiltshire was secured. He later said that he had intended to disable the warder and get his keys off him, then go in search of his companion on the night of the murder, whose evidence had condemned him, and kill him. Despite this incident, Wiltshire was reprieved soon afterwards and his death sentence was commuted to life imprisonment.

In February 1882, seventeen-year-old Oliver Selwyn was let into one of the airing yards for exercise and was left there unattended. He stacked up a pile of coils of oakum and placed an old stretcher on top, which he used to get over the yard wall. From there, he managed to climb over the boundary wall and made his escape. He was pursued by the police, and was finally caught in Newent. He had been committed about ten days previously on charges of stealing a bicycle and a horse.

One morning in September 1895, convict Albert Edward Harman was working in one of the yards when he saw an opportunity to escape. He ran up a ladder which had been left unattended, scaled the wall and dropped into the gardens of the governor's house, then made for the docks. The hue and cry was raised and the police were requested to keep a look-out for Harman, who was well-known in the city. It was reported that he had been seen in Gloucester that morning, trying to exchange his prison clothes for ordinary attire. It was also rumoured that he was spotted at the docks in the evening.

Late that same night, a dock constable encountered Harman in the Dock Company's ballast yard, close to Llanthony Bridge. Harman struck him with an iron bar, then ran away. The constable blew his whistle, and warders, policemen and some civilians came to see what was happening. The search continued, but the trail was lost, and Harman was not recaptured.

On 25 October 1906, an escape from Gloucester Prison made national headlines. In an episode which was described as a 'prison mutiny', eleven convicts in the Separate Prison got out of their cells and five of them escaped completely.

At the end of the working day, two prison officers were going from cell to cell, collecting the work each prisoner had completed. Michael Harnett, known as 'London Mike', and another prisoner attacked the officers when their cell doors were unlocked, hitting one of them hard in the face. The injured officer and his colleague struggled with the men for some time, but eventually they were overpowered and the prisoners took their keys and locked them in the cells, before starting to let out other prisoners. The governor, Mr Finn, who came to investigate the commotion, also was locked in a cell, and was rumoured to have had his watch stolen.

The men ran to the gatehouse, where they grabbed the porter and took his keys, then unlocked the outside door. Six prisoners were stopped from getting out by other staff members who had been alerted by the cries of the officers and the governor (and according to some reports, by the governor's wife ringing the prison bell), but five, including London Mike, got away.

Once outside, the men commandeered a boat and forced its owner to row them across the river, then ran off. One of the convicts soon got tired and gave himself up to a railway signalman. The others made for the Forest of Dean, where they were apprehended the following afternoon, very tired and hungry, and were sent by train from Lydney back to Gloucester, escorted by a party of policemen and prison officers.

A week after the incident, the Visiting Justices held a private inquiry at the prison, to discuss what had happened. One of the officers who had been overpowered by the prisoners was too badly injured to attend, so the meeting was adjourned for a week. It transpired that when the officers were going from cell to cell, two doors mistakenly had been unlocked at the same time, which had allowed their occupants to make their attack.

One newspaper commented that it was well known that Gloucester Prison had been 'notoriously understaffed' since the authorities began using it as a convict prison. Questions were asked in the House of Commons about staffing levels at Gloucester, but the Home Secretary responded that the mutiny had happened due to the officers unlocking two doors at the same time, not because there weren't enough staff.

During the construction of a terrace of prison officers' houses in 1923, prisoner George Smith, who was working in the exercise yard on the afternoon of 25 October, disappeared. Smith had been serving a sentence of one month's imprisonment for deserting his wife. He had been due for release that day, but he knew that as soon as he came out, he was going to be arrested by Shropshire police on a charge of false pretences. It was believed that Smith had managed to get hold of a civilian worker's coat which he put on over his prison uniform, then either walked out with other workers, or got into a lorry which had come in to deliver building materials.

Because Smith's sentence at Gloucester had expired on the day he disappeared, the prison authorities had no jurisdiction over him, unless the Prison Commissioners made out a special order for his arrest, so it was up to the Shropshire police to pursue him. A few days after Smith's disappearance, a parcel of prison clothes was found in a train when it stopped at Gloucester station, addressed to H.M. Prison Gloucester.

In January 1927, a prisoner named Cuves who was being treated in Gloucester's Royal Infirmary managed to escape, dressed only in a nightshirt. The *Cheltenham Chronicle* reported that 'an exciting chase' had taken place on the evening of 16 January. Cuves, who was well enough to walk about the ward, had asked to go to the lavatory. From there, he climbed onto a balcony and got down a fire escape.

He was spotted in the hospital grounds; the alarm was raised and he was chased by porters and doctors. He ran across the grounds and scaled a wall, dropping into the garden of a house in Brunswick Square. Making his way along the row of gardens, he eventually found a house with an unlocked back door and passed through the house, out of the front door and into the street. Police and warders found the exhausted prisoner about half an hour later, walking up Southgate Street. He was taken to the prison's own infirmary.

In the early hours of 13 July 1942, prisoner Edward William Hunt escaped from Gloucester Prison, in order to visit his wife and new-born son in Cheltenham Hospital. Hunt was a tiler and slater by trade, who had been lodging in Cheltenham with his wife when he was arrested on charges of committing forgery. He was tried at the Gloucestershire Assizes for obtaining money using forged cheques and Post Office savings books, and was sentenced to four years' penal servitude.

It was discovered that Hunt had managed to bore a hole through the wall of his cell, through which he got into the prison yard. He used a rope to climb over the boundary wall, then made his way to Cheltenham on a prison officer's bicycle. As the bicycle had been in the prison yard, it was presumed that Hunt must have hauled it over the wall with him. Because he was wearing brown overalls on top of his prison uniform, he was able to visit his wife and son twice before the hospital staff realised that he was an escaped prisoner.

Hunt was captured in Manchester in early August, after he was arrested for obtaining £3 by false pretences from the Post Office, using four cheques he had stolen from a house in Birmingham. He was sent to Birmingham to be tried for housebreaking, and in December he was sentenced to serve another eighteen months' hard labour for his latest offences, on top of his original four year sentence.

Two escapes from Gloucester Prison took place in 1947. On the morning of 18 March, Albert Trevor Rogers, who was serving two years for shop-breaking and larceny, went missing. He was understood to have climbed a rope over the wall into Barbican Alley, wearing his prison uniform of a grey jacket and trousers. Nothing more was seen of Rogers until May, when he was arrested in Liverpool and appeared at the city magistrates court there for stealing clothing and food worth £60.

The second escape was of a prisoner who was in an outside working party. Albert Williams, a forty-eight-year-old collier from Abergavenny, was one of a working party employed at Smith's Farm, near Pendock, when he went missing on 15 August. A description was issued by the police, and a reward offered by the Gloucester Prison authorities, for information leading to his apprehension. At the end of August, there was still no trace of Williams, and police throughout the country were looking for him. As far as is known, he was not recaptured.

Exterior wall of B Wing, part of the 'Separate Prison', opened in 1850. (Jill Evans, 2017)

7

EXECUTIONS

In the eighteenth century, most British prisons carried out executions of prisoners sentenced to death at their local Assizes. At Gloucester, those who had committed crimes within the city boundaries were executed outside the city gaol. When the county gaol was in the old castle, those sentenced to death by the County Assizes were taken to the hamlet of Over, north-west of the city, to be hanged. When the new county prison was designed, the opportunity was taken to build the gatehouse with a flat roof, so that executions could be held on it, giving a good view to spectators.

In the late eighteenth and early nineteenth centuries, many crimes other than murder were capital offences, including housebreaking and burglary, the theft of horses, cattle and sheep, arson and highway robbery. This meant that a large number of mandatory death sentences were given out at the Assizes, resulting in the gaol's condemned cells being crammed with prisoners, but most of those who had been condemned were reprieved a few days later.

The unlucky few who were left to die would receive regular visits from the prison chaplain, who would endeavour to offer spiritual comfort, but also would try to get the prisoners to admit that they had committed the offences for which they were condemned, and to acknowledge the justice of their sentences. If the prisoner was of a denomination other than the Church of England, a clergyman of the same denomination would be asked to attend the prisoner. William Davis, who was hanged in 1839, was accompanied to the scaffold by a Wesleyan minister, as well as the prison chaplain.

It was written into the 1790 rules of Gloucester Prison that executions should take place on 'Saturday fortnight after the Assizes', unless another date had been fixed. This would have applied to prisoners who had committed crimes other than murder, as murderers usually were executed only two days after their trials.

On the day of the execution, a special service would be held in the chapel, attended by all the prisoners, including the condemned man or woman. The chaplain also would attend the prisoner privately in the condemned cell. When the time came, the chaplain would accompany the prisoner to the scaffold. The execution would be attended by the County High Sheriff, who was responsible for overseeing executions, the prison surgeon, and various other officials.

After the execution had taken place, the prisoner would be left hanging for an hour, after which he or she would be cut down and placed in an open coffin. A coroner's inquest would be held soon after, at which the inquest jury had to view the body. The governor would confirm the identity of the deceased prisoner and the surgeon would state that he had examined the body and declared life extinct.

Once the formalities had been completed, the bodies of those who had committed crimes other than murder could be taken away by family or friends and buried in their home parishes. Only murderers could not be interred in consecrated ground. Until 1832, murderers usually were sent to the local infirmary to be anatomised. It can be presumed that non-murderers whose bodies had not been claimed by family or friends would be sent for dissection too.

In 1832, it became law that judges passing sentence of death on murderers must order that their bodies be buried within the prison grounds. At Gloucester, prisoners seem to have been buried in various areas of the prison up to 1864; after that, there was a place in the yard designated for the burial of the bodies.

The first execution at the new prison was supposed to be held on 15 August 1791, after William Birt was sentenced to death at Gloucestershire's Summer Assizes, but he hanged himself in his cell on 13 August. After the following Assizes, held in April 1792, Charles Rackford and John Hughes were sentenced to death for committing highway robbery. Their executions took place on 14 April.

A portable scaffold with a collapsing platform was erected on the gatehouse roof for the executions. The two men were Roman Catholics and were attended by a priest of that faith. While a large crowd gathered outside, all of the criminal prisoners were made to watch the execution, from inside the prison's walls. The spectators had a long wait before they saw the pair dispatched, as it was five hours before they finished their devotions and gave the signal that they were ready to die.

At Gloucester, it was common for at least one execution to take place per year, up until the mid-nineteenth century. In some years, multiple hangings would be witnessed by the crowds who gathered on such occasions. On 28 April 1827, five men were hanged together on the gatehouse roof. Those executed included nineteen-year-old Joseph Ray, who had been condemned for committing burglary. The chaplain recorded that during the service in the prison chapel on the morning of the executions, Ray was so distressed that he had to be carried out in a fit.

During 1826, work began to build a new gatehouse, in the north-east wall of the prison. Once building work had been completed, executions took place on the new gatehouse roof. It isn't clear when the first execution was held there, but the earliest mention in the press of the new gatehouse being used was on 18 April 1829, when brothers Henry and Matthew Pinnell were hanged together for committing highway robbery.

The *Gloucester Journal* reported that 'an immense concourse of persons assembled in front of the new entrance to the county gaol', and that the brothers 'ascended the platform, which was erected over the new lodge in front of the prison, at a quarter past twelve o'clock'.

By the 1830s, when most of the crimes which previously had been capital offences had been removed from the statute book, the frequency of executions held at Gloucester Prison fell. On 20 April 1839, William Davis was hanged for committing murder, watched by an immense crowd. After that, there were no more executions at Gloucester Prison for twenty-five years.

The 1820s gatehouse. (Jill Evans, 2013)

When Lewis Gough was sentenced to death for murder at the Summer Assizes in 1864, he was held in a room in the prison infirmary. This was probably because after a long period with no executions, the prison had started to use the condemned cells for other purposes. Gough was hanged on 27 August 1864, by William Calcraft.

The *Gloucester Journal* of 3 September 1864 gave a detailed account of the execution. Shortly after seven o'clock in the morning, the report said, Gough was taken from his cell and escorted to the front lobby of the old gaol, where he was delivered into the custody of the High Sheriff. Calcraft pinioned his arms, then a procession made its way to the scaffold, consisting of the prisoner, the executioner, the High Sheriff, the

Under Sheriffs, the chaplain (Mr Dudley), the surgeon (Mr Hickes), and two warders.

At about five minutes past seven, the party arrived on the gatehouse roof, in sight of the multitude of spectators gathered in the square in front of the prison. The bell ceased tolling and the crowd fell silent. Gough addressed the spectators, warning them to avoid 'drunkenness and covetousness'. The chaplain offered up a prayer, then the prisoner, who was in tears, began to ascend the steps to the platform. Because he was lame in one leg, a warder and the executioner helped him. Calcraft put a white hood over Gough's head and placed the noose round his neck, before strapping his feet. Then Calcraft climbed down, leaving Gough alone for a few seconds, before the drop fell with a heavy thud.

After Gough had been hanging for an hour, Calcraft returned to cut him down and then an inquest was held. At about midday, he was buried, fully dressed, in a makeshift plot at the back of the Debtors' Prison.

This was the last execution to be held on the gatehouse roof, because in 1868, it became law that executions must take place inside a prison's walls. In total, between 1792 and 1864, 104 public executions had been held at the county gaol.

The first execution inside the walls of Gloucester Prison took place on 8 January 1872, when Frederick Jones was hanged for murdering his sweetheart. Jones was dispatched in the prison yard, by William Calcraft. A notice that the execution had been carried out successfully was pinned onto the prison gates, after the coroner's inquest had been held.

In January 1874, a triple execution took place at Gloucester Prison. Charles Butt had been sentenced to death for killing a young woman with whom he was infatuated, while Edwin Bailey and Ann Barry had murdered Bailey's illegitimate daughter. The three were hanged together in the prison yard on 27 January, at eight o'clock in the morning. The executioner was meant to have been William Calcraft, but he was ill, so Robert Anderson took his place. Concerns were raised after the event that although the execution was supposed to be held in private, about fifty 'guests' had attended it.

Seven more executions were carried out in one of the yards at Gloucester Prison, until in 1912, a new execution chamber was built onto the end of the wall of A Wing, in order to fulfil new government regulations. The condemned cell was placed at the end of A Wing and a set of double doors was knocked through the outside wall, connecting it to the new chamber.

When the prisoner's time came, the doors were opened and the executioner would come in and pinion him. Then he was taken through to the chamber and stood on a set of trap doors. When the bolt was drawn, the doors collapsed and the body dropped down into a lower room, where it was left hanging for the customary hour. Gilbert Oswald Smith, who had murdered his wife at Uley, was the first prisoner to be hanged in the new execution chamber, on 26 November 1912.

The *Cheltenham Chronicle* commented that 'the scene outside the gaol was in striking contrast to that at previous executions, when the Barrack-square has been crowded with noisy people, many of whom took up a position near the walls in the hope of hearing the thud of the drop platform on the drawing of the lever, and of seeing the black flag hoisted.'

The *Gloucester Journal* reported that 'Smith was the first culprit to be hanged in the new death chamber, which is quite a small room, admitting of the presence of a very small number of people indeed.' Thanks to the proximity of the new scaffold to the condemned cell, which was 'barely half a dozen paces distant', the prisoner was 'spared the infliction of anything approaching a parade to the scaffold'.

Members of the press were not allowed to view the body on this occasion. The *Gloucester Journal* report said that at earlier executions at which the press had been present, the bodies of executed criminals were placed in their coffins and left in the execution yard pending inspection by the inquest jury, so anyone else attending the execution could see the body. On this occasion, Smith's body was placed on a slab in a cell and 'the jury saw nothing of the scaffold'.

By the 1920s, many local prisons either had closed down or no longer carried out executions. Gloucester was one of the remaining 'Hanging Prisons', and as such it now carried out executions of prisoners from areas outside Gloucestershire. This meant that in 1922, when Hay-on-Wye solicitor Herbert Rowse Armstrong was sentenced to death at the Hereford Assizes for murdering his wife, it was ordered that he should be hanged at Gloucester Prison. His execution took place on 31 May 1922, while a massive crowd stood outside the prison gates.

The last execution ever to be held at Gloucester Prison took place on 7 June 1939, when Ralph Smith was hanged for murdering his landlady and former lover, in Swindon. His trial took place at the Old Bailey in London, but Gloucester Prison was chosen as the place where he would die. The executioner was Thomas Pierrepoint, assisted by his brother Albert.

The execution chamber was kept in readiness at Gloucester until the 1960s, when capital punishment was effectively abolished. In total, 121 prisoners - 112 men and 9 women - were executed at Gloucester's county prison between 1791 and 1939.

The faint outline of the 1912 execution chamber, on the end wall of A Wing. (Jill Evans, 2013)

CONCLUSION

After 1950, H.M.P. Gloucester continued for another sixty-three years, expanding and adapting in an effort to meet the needs of the modern penal system, but confined by its limited space. In the 1960s, a new cell block, named C Wing, was built east of the Victorian building which housed A and B Wings, and a unit for young offenders was added in the 1970s.

In the mid-1980s, major reconstruction at the west side of the prison complex took place, with the building of a new entrance, reception and administration block. Gloucester Prison in the modern era was a Category B adult male local prison and young offender institution. Most of its prisoners were on remand, awaiting trial or in the early stage of a sentence.

A number of the surviving older structures were given listed status in the 1970s. These are detailed on the website of Historic England, and their descriptions include some useful information on how the prison buildings were used in later years.

The Victorian prison block (originally the 'Separate Prison'), incorporating the 1790s entrance to the gatehouse, and containing A and B Wings and the chapel, is Grade II* listed. The original iron stairways and the balconies, with their unusual serpent and lion's paw designs, are included in the listing. Various structures had been added to the building in the latter half of the twentieth century, including a footbridge to the modern cell block at the front and a kitchen block and boiler room to the rear of the chapel.

Some of the cells in A and B Wings had been knocked together to make larger rooms. Most of the original Victorian cell doors had been replaced. In the twentieth century, some cell walls had been removed to provide communal washing areas. The chapel roof had been replaced, and the ground floor area of the chapel, originally an open space with Doric columns supporting the upper floor, had been subdivided into rooms, incorporating the columns.

The 1826 gatehouse is Grade II listed. Some interior alterations took place in 1993, when the gatehouse was converted into a prison museum. The central passageway, containing arched gates to the front and rear, was enclosed and a first floor inserted. (The report does not include the information that in the last few years of H.M.P. Gloucester, the gatehouse was used as a Visitor Centre and Family Support Centre, for visitors to prisoners, who brought young families with them.)

The Debtors' Prison, built in 1826, is Grade II listed. The building had become unsafe by the late twentieth century, so its third floor was removed and the roof was replaced. Part of the building was converted into offices, but some of the original structures and features survived, including a 'top section of a re-used Blackburn-era turnstile' and some interior walls on the ground floor, plus some former cells on the first floor.

The governor's house, built in 1863, is Grade II listed, as are the iron railings at its front. By the 1970s, the house had become the prison officers' mess and training centre. The part of the boundary wall running along Barbican Road, between the 1826 gatehouse and the governor's house, also is Grade II listed.

The last report of H.M.P. Gloucester's Independent Monitoring Board, published in 2013, also contained some information on changes which had taken place since 1950.

The building which held A and B Wings continued to be used, usually with two prisoners being held in each cell, although originally they had been designed to hold one person. These cells had washing and toilet facilities in them. The Segregation Unit and Vulnerable Prisoners' Unit had been housed in B Wing. After the young offenders' unit was closed down, young prisoners usually were held in B Wing too. C Wing, built in the 1960s, consisted of single cells, without toilet facilities within.

The former chapel, at the rear of A and B Wings, had been converted to provide facilities for prisoner induction, basic learning skills assessments, etc. A new chapel, incorporating a multi-faith room and office, had been provided by converting the former main storeroom.

The kitchen was situated adjacent to A and B Wings. Other, separate buildings included a two-storey healthcare centre and a Learning Skills centre. Another building had been used as a recycling centre, with an Offender Management Unit on the upper floor. A bicycle repair shop was situated in the former staff rest-room. There was a gymnasium, and three exercise yards, the main one being used for basketball and volley ball.

Between 3 and 13 July 2012, Her Majesty's Chief Inspector of Prisons carried out an unannounced inspection at H.M.P. Gloucester. A report on the findings of the inspection was published later that year. In the introduction, it was stated that 'Gloucester is one of the older establishments in the prison system, with a poor infrastructure and situated in a cramped inner city location. Overall this is not a good report, with many issues and concerns we have raised in previous reports still to be addressed.'

The Prison Inspectorate said that the accommodation at Gloucester was 'among the poorest in the prison system'. Cells in A and B Wings, mostly holding two occupants, were 'dark and dingy and invariably overcrowded'. Apart from their beds, prisoners had to share the furniture in their cells, due to lack of space. The toilets in shared cells were inadequately screened.

In C Wing, a 'night sanitation' system was in operation, in which cells were unlocked remotely and electronically when occupants needed access to the toilet at night. Only one prisoner could be let out at a time, so there was often a wait of up to two hours, which meant the system was 'flawed and demeaning'.

The quality of the regime at Gloucester was considered poor, with over half of prisoners being locked in their cells for most of the day and having very little to keep them occupied. The range of educational and vocational opportunities was judged to be inadequate.

Points in the prison's favour were the quality of prisoner-staff relations and the fact that most prisoners at Gloucester regarded it as being a safe place. Since the last report, there had been relatively few incidents of violence, but there had been two cases of 'self-destruction'. The report also praised the quality of the food, the library service, the physical education regime and the provision of health care. Overall though, the problems at H.M.P. Gloucester were considered to be 'fundamental'.

After the publication of this report, rumours circulated that Gloucester Prison was going to be shut down. In January 2013, it was announced that H.M.P. Gloucester was going to close, along with several other older local prisons. The relocation of prisoners began almost immediately, and Gloucester Prison closed, after nearly 222 years of continuous operation, on 31 March 2013.

A cell in A Wing, designed for one person, but occupied by two inmates in the last days of the prison. (Jill Evans, 2013)

SOURCES

Original Records at Gloucestershire Archives:

Gloucester County Gaol:

Prison Chaplain's Journals (Q/Gc31)

Prison Governor's Journals (Q/Gc3)

Prison Surgeon's Journals (Q/Gc32)

Visiting Justices' Journals (Q/Gc1)

Printed records at Gloucestershire Archives:

Extract from Holford, G., *Report of the Committee of the House of Commons on the Laws Relating to Penitentiary Houses*, 1811, pp.19-30

Extract from *Report of the Select Committee on the State of the Gaols*, 1819, pp.388-405

Rules and Bye-laws for Gloucester Gaol and Penitentiary, published 1790

Rules and Regulations for Gloucester Gaol and Penitentiary, published 1809

Rules for the Government of the Gaol and Penitentiary and the Houses of Correction for the County of Gloucester, published 1837

White, B., *The Murderers of Gloucestershire, 1872-1939* (Home Office, H.M. Prison Service, 1985).

Other printed records:

Howard, John, *The State of the Prisons in England and Wales*, 3rd edn., 1784

Neild, James, *The State of the Prisons in England, Wales and Scotland*, 1812

Newspapers

Cheltenham Chronicle

The Citizen

Gloucestershire Echo

Gloucester Journal

Books

Baker, B., and Butler, L., eds., *The Prison Service in Britain* (Tempus, 2006)

Evans, Jill, *Hanged at Gloucester* (The History Press, 2011)

Herbert, N.M., ed., *A History of the County of Gloucester, Volume IV, City of Gloucester* (Victoria County History, 1988)

Higgs, Michelle, *Prison Life in Victorian England* (Tempus, 2007)

Jack, Elizabeth, *Victorian Prisoners of Gloucester Gaol: A Rogues' Gallery* (The History Press, 2009)

Morris, N. and Rothman, D.J., eds., *The Oxford History of the Prison* (OUP, 1998)

Priestley, P., *Victorian Prison Lives* (Pimlico, 1999)

Whiting, J.R.S., *Prison Reform in Gloucestershire, 1776-1820* (Phillimore, 1975)

Websites

British Newspaper Archive (britishnewspaperarchive.co.uk)

H.M. Prison Inspectorate, Inspection of H.M.P. Gloucester, 3-13 July 2012 (justiceinspectorates.gov.uk)

Independent Monitoring Board, Report on H.M.P. Gloucester, 2011-13 (imb.org.uk)

Listed buildings, list entry nos. 1245472-6 and 1271654 (historicengland.org.uk/listing/thelist)

INDEX

By the same author

Hanged at Gloucester (The History Press, 2011)
The Gloucester Book of Days (The History Press, 2013)
Gloucester Murder & Crime (The History Press, 2013)

Gloucestershire Crime History blog:
www.gloscrimehistory.wordpress.com

Facebook pages:
www.facebook.com/gloscrimehistory
www.facebook.com/booksbyjillevans